The Temptation of Biology:
Freud's Theories of Sexuality

followed by

Biologism and Biology

The Temptation of Biology: Freud's Theories of Sexuality

followed by

Biologism and Biology

Jean Laplanche

Translated by Donald Nicholson-Smith

New York:
The Unconscious in Translation

Originally published as *Le Fourvoiement biologisant de la
sexualité chez Freud* (Paris: Synthélabo, 1993); second edition,
with annexed talk of October 23, 1997: *La Sexualité humaine
+ Biologisme et biologie* (Paris: Synthélabo, 1999); third edition
(unchanged): *Problématiques VII: Le Fourvoiement biologisant
de la sexualité chez Freud, suivi de "Biologisme et biologie"*
(Paris: Presses Universitaires de France, 2006).

Cover art: *Jules Being Dried by His Mother*, 1900
oil painting by Mary Cassatt (American, 1844–1926)

ISBN 978-1-942254-01-0
Library of Congress Control Number: 2014951267

CONTENTS

II. Biologism and Biology 113

Translator's Acknowledgments

I am most grateful to Jonathan House, editor and publisher of this series of translations of the work of the late Jean Laplanche, for giving me the opportunity, as a translator, to revisit Laplanche, for whose magisterial conceptual concordance to Freud, *Vocabulaire de la psych-analyse*, written in collaboration with J.-B. Pontalis, I prepared an English version entitled *The Language of Psychoanalysis* in the early 1970s.

I must further acknowledge, naturally, the support of the Fondation Laplanche, under whose aegis these translations into English are being commissioned and published.

For editorial advice and help I am indebted, once again, to Jonathan House, whose assistance has been invaluable and unstinting. I have also benefited from scrupulous reading and copyediting of the manuscript by Michael Farrin and Andrew Baird, and they have my great thanks.

Mia Nadezhda Rublowska has provided invaluable guidance, but I have to thank her, as ever, for very much more than that.

D. N.-S.

Prefatory Note to *Problématiques I–VII*

From 1962 at the École Normale Supérieure and the Sorbonne, and from 1969 at the Teaching and Research Unit (UER) in Clinical Human Sciences (Sorbonne/Paris University VII), my public teaching took a problematizing and interpretative path along a few major axes of psychoanalytical theory. My lectures from the academic year 1970–1971 onward have been collected in seven volumes under the general title of *Problématiques*.* My spoken words have been altered only to the extent necessitated by their transposition to print.

The themes of the successive years follow a sequence answering to no decided logic, the order being governed partly by content and partly by my own development. Only after the fact did I realize that it might not be too artificial to gather my lectures together in a series of volumes.

Depending on their personal disposition and receptiveness, readers may react in two ways. In response to the apparent classicism of the ideas and my frequent recourse to critical glosses of Freudian texts, and to the recapitulation and repetition that are unavoidable when one is addressing a largely new audience every year, some may well dismiss these transcripts as an extreme example of the widely decried fad for "Freudian" exegesis. Others, I hope, will summon sufficient patience and generosity to get in step with me and even perhaps appreciate the ways in which I have enhanced Freud's thinking or broken new ground by placing considerable stress on dividing lines or by reorienting concepts. I have continually striven, in every sense, to "put Freudian thought to work."

Three key notions may help illuminate my theoretical enterprise and the "faithful infidelity" that has guided me as a principle in pursuing it. Those notions are "exigency," the "spiral," and "going-astray."

When I speak of *exigency* I am referring not to the exigency of Freud as a thinker, as rigorous as he might have been, but to the exigency of his object, the imperious object which fascinated him from his earliest work until the end of his life. That object was quite simply the unconscious, whose existence is undeniable but which can never be completely apprehended. We can nevertheless say certain things about it, notably that it is incontestably sexual in nature.

As for the *spiral*, it is a curve swirling around a fixed point that attracts it. The pathway of a thought returning at regular intervals to review the same problem; at each visit the problem becomes more elaborate, or may even change in its contours, and each circuit of the issue emancipates itself from the last, implying a step forward.

Finally, *going-astray (le fourvoiement)* is inseparable from exigency, and indeed is a consequence thereof. A mountain climber fixated on the summit but lost in the mist may suddenly take a wrong turn and find himself at an impasse. Should he carry on regardless or retrace his steps to the fork in the road? And at what cost?

Identifying and describing such goings-astray can lead to a clearer picture of fundamental problematics often difficult to discern in the conceptual labyrinth. This way of problematizing a doctrine that has too often been talked to death allows a fresh, stripped-down theme to emerge—the theme I have proposed to call the "general theory of seduction."

J. L.

---

* I. *L'Angoisse* (1970–73), Paris: PUF, 1980; II. *Castration et symbolisations* (1973–75), Paris: PUF, 1980; III. *La Sublimation* (1975–77), Paris: PUF, 1980; IV. *L'Inconscient et le ça* (1977–79), Paris: PUF, 1981; V. *Le Baquet; La Transcendance du transfert* (1979–84), Paris: PUF, 1987; VI. *L'Après-coup* (1989–90), Paris: PUF, 2006.

I

The Temptation of Biology: Freud's Theories of Sexuality

Lectures (1991–92) for the Diplôme des Études
Approfondies (DEA) in Psychoanalysis,
University of Paris VII, X, and XIII.

Preface

In 1970, in *Life and Death in Psychoanalysis*,[1] I developed the idea of sexuality "leaning-on" (*Anlehnung*) the self-preservative functions. At that time the concept of seduction was already part of my thinking, and subsequently it came to occupy a more and more central place. After *New Foundations for Psychoanalysis* (1987),[2] it became necessary for me once again to follow in Freud's footsteps through what I call his biologizing going-astray.

Once Freud abandoned the seduction theory, a return to a purely endogenous theory of sexuality became unavoidable: although he had initially rejected the notion of instinct anchored in phylogenesis, this notion never ceased to haunt his thought thereafter.

I shall be addressing three instances of this going-astray in Freud's work:

(1) The theory of leaning-on, which posits a sexuality that emerges by supporting itself or leaning on self-preservation. Very little elaborated by Freud, this theory cannot in our view survive a purely endogenous interpretation. Its internal contradictions, which I analyze at length, stem from what the theory omits: the splitting-off

---

1 *Vie et mort en psychanalyse* (Paris: Flammarion, 1970); Eng. trans. by Jeffrey Mehlman: *Life and Death in Psychoanalysis* (Baltimore and London: Johns Hopkins University Press, 1976 [hereafter *Life and Death*]).
2 *Nouveaux fondements pour la psychanalyse* (Paris: PUF, 1987); Eng. trans. by David Macey: *New Foundations for Psychoanalysis* (Oxford: Blackwell, 1989 [hereafter *New Foundations*]). A new English translation by Robert Stein is to be published by The Unconscious in Translation.

of a properly sexual realm from the biology of childhood is inconceivable without a basis in *the action of the other person*.

(2) With "On Narcissism: An Introduction" (1915), Freud opened up the possibility of a fruitful theoretical revision by clearly distinguishing three levels: the self-preservative, the sexual-erotic, and the sexual-narcissistic. He even evoked the action of the adult other as the starting point of the sexual object-choice.

(3) Very soon afterwards, however, these indispensable distinctions were dissolved by the advent of Freud's final theory of the drives. What Freud now proposed under the heading of a unifying Eros was ultimately the return of instinct in a mythical guise. Admittedly, the "death drive" was introduced in order to preserve psychic conflict, but this was a hybrid concept in which Freud and his successors refused to discern the return of a "demonic" sexuality. Once the historical function of this concept has been fully grasped—its function as a compensation for the initial straying—psychoanalysis will be well advised to get rid of it.

Exposing Freud's biologizing tendencies by no means implies a dismissal of biology's role in the human being.[3] On the contrary, it restores biology to a positive place, a place that is no longer mythological; and it opens the door to exacting research into the way in which fantasies can invest, divert, and indeed "shore up" the functioning of that biology which human ethology is now beginning to describe more accurately.

---

3 The term "biologizing" may have opened the door to misunderstandings. I do not disparage biology, but merely the genetic, hereditary, phylogenetic theory that has persistently dominated Freudian metapsychology ever since Freud's abandonment of the seduction theory.

November 19, 1991

Freud as the initiator of Freudianism's going-astray

This year I intend to demarcate my subject by using the title "Strayings of Freudianism" or "Strayings of Freudian Thought." What I imply by this is that I want to challenge not just Freudians but also Freud himself: strayings by Freud and by those in his wake.

From two very different quarters—but in agreement on this point—I have recently been accused of being a *revisionist*. This term, with its stale whiff of Stalinism, makes me smile. I will name no names, but I refuse this stigma, for what I am trying to do is something other than revision. You revise a paper, a text, but there is no question of revising Freud.

I have been reproached for endangering the *equilibrium* of Freudian thought, which immediately raises the question of what such an equilibrium—that of any body of thought, and that of Freudian thought in particular—might be like. Like a building, a fine building, from which no wing, no part, should be removed? Must we accept it en bloc under penalty of being a deviationist, just as for centuries Aristotelianism has been respected, or as in certain circles even today Holy Scripture is treated? Are we Talmudists?

Is Freudian thought a fine building in that sense? Must we either accept it as a whole or choose an alternative? Obviously, the answer is neither. For my part I would say that one must be acquainted with Freud's entire work, but also be able, precisely by virtue of that acquaintanceship, to discern the *false* equilibria within it, the unstable equilibria, the compensations, and to take a pickaxe or the knife to those cracks.

Freud himself accused his dissenters, Jung or Adler—his two great demons, hardly deserving, truth to tell, of this honor or this indignity—of stressing one or another aspect of his thought in a unilateral way. And indeed, it is certain that accentuating one side of Freud to the detriment of the other, ignoring what the two signify when taken together, produces a completely inadequate view.

So what does it mean to "interpret Freud with Freud" (to borrow the title of an article of mine[4])? Certainly not to turn Freud's thought into a hermeneutics, which would be to transpose his work into another system deemed superior to his—as Jung sought to do along with several others, including perhaps, in a way, Lacan. This means forgetting Freud's own distrust of systems—of all systems.

Nor does interpreting Freud with Freud mean psychoanalyzing Freud, which some authors have attempted to do with varying degrees of success.[5] I do not believe that a psychoanalysis of Freud is likely to get me where I wish to go.

Interpreting Freud: on the track of exigency, guided by the source-object

I think there is a level of interpretation at which one can trace something in Freud that I have long called exigency. Exigency in this sense is something dictated by the object: not by Freud the man, nor by logic. In a way, and notably in the case of the psychoanalytic method, it is the "unconscious" object itself that guides the development of thought. In terms of exigency, interpreting Freud with Freud

---

4 "Interpréter [avec] Freud," *L'Arc* 34 (1968). Reprinted in *La révolution copernicienne inachevée. Travaux 1967–1992* (Paris: Aubier, 1992 [hereafter *Révolution copernicienne*]), pp. 21–36.
5 See for example the remarkable work of Didier Anzieu.

means dismantling and, mutatis mutandis, adapting Freud's own rules of disassembly in such a way that eventually things come back together in a different way before our eyes, precisely as a result of the object's exigency. As in a psychoanalysis, such interpretation implies the uncovering of the subterranean forces that govern plainly visible revisions, and hence at certain moments reveals a sort of crypto-Freud masked by the official one. I have noted more than once how Freud, in writing his own history, managed to cover or embellish his tracks.[6]

What is meant by returning to the source? A crypto-Freud is certainly not a proto-Freud. It is not a matter of going in search of an early Freud in the way that an early Marx or an early Hegel has been said to be more authentic than a later one. Though it may be true that at times an earlier Freud is closer to what I call exigency than the later, this is no reason to argue that the later never came close to it. We are not talking, therefore, about a return to the source in a temporal sense. Hölderlin says that as it nears its estuary the river approaches its source: a dialectical thought, strongly marked by the poet's familiarity with Hegel. Well, things are a little like that here: we are not looking to unearth "sources," or some illusory "first," but rather to find what constitutes the source and keeps getting covered up, just as a stream suddenly gets lost in its meanderings, becoming for a time what is known as a "losing stream," only to reconstitute itself later after a period of underground dispersal. This is what we are concerned with: the source of inspiration is nothing but the object of the quest.

I have proposed the idea of straying, implying that the search of the one who strays is guided by a persistent aim. Someone who wishes to reach the top of Mount Everest and who goes astray, coming all of a sudden upon a cliff, is clearly still guided by the mountain, pushed on by his idea of the summit. This implies the exigency of

---

6 A good example of our way of uncovering a crypto-Freud, not an esoteric Freud but rather the Freud of a subterranean tendency that is continually being covered up, is Jacques André's "La sexualité féminine, retour aux sources," *Psychanalyse à l'Université*, vol. 16 (1991), no. 62, pp. 5–50.

arriving somewhere. In very concrete terms, it further implies forks in the road, possible choices, and occasionally the choice of a dead end. And of course it does not suffice to have the thinking process go into reverse and return as it were to the crossroads and take the right direction, the royal road. For with a thinker such as Freud, an impasse is never absolute, since the seeker is still being guided by his main object; in other words, to return to the analogy of the mountaineer reaching an insurmountable cliff, he is liable to find other paths, ever drawn on by the exigency of the summit, without necessarily returning to the fork.

Moreover, the claim is not that there is nothing new in Freudian thought. New discoveries occur as clinical experience and methodology advance, and they serve to complicate the whole picture. From the moment a thought, though still governed by the exigency of its source-object, has nevertheless committed itself to something that resembles a significant straying from the path (even perhaps at the outset, although I have my reservations about the idea of errors that are "initial" in a temporal sense)—from that moment, compensations intended to incorporate fresh facts and reopen a way to the mountaintop often take the form of ad hoc hypotheses, which is to say hypotheses invented to meet the needs of the moment and to get the new facts into harmony with a theory that does not necessarily accord with them.[7]

The demonstration of a straying certainly involves exposing the error, the wrong turn, but it also means trying to show the cause of the error, and that is where the issue gets complicated: no straying

---

7 The notion of the ad hoc auxiliary hypothesis in this sense is advanced notably by Karl Popper. A theory that is contradicted by certain facts may be made more complex by the addition of new hypotheses rather than being replaced by a simpler and more general hypothesis. Ad hoc hypotheses are to be found in certain very muddled texts of Freud's. Could the death drive perhaps be described as an ad hoc hypothesis? Freud's genius, characterized as it is by inventiveness and openness to new facts, is also prone to balk at any re-examination of a fundamentally wrong path taken.

is innocent, none is without a cause; but how can we get our bearings when it is still, and always, the *object* that is the main cause of the straying—the main cause not only of the true exigency, but also of deviations and dead ends on the way to the truth?

"Theoretico-genesis recapitulates ontogenesis"

There is a covering up of sexuality and the unconscious in Freud's own work that parallels the covering up of sexuality and the unconscious in the human being. This is something I have tried to express by parodying Haeckel's law, which holds that "ontogenesis recapitulates phylogenesis," by saying that "theoretico-genesis," here meaning the actual development of theory with its changing forms, tends to recapitulate ontogenesis, i.e. the fate of sexuality and the unconscious in the human being.

To the trajectory of Freud's work, and complicating matters still further, I am duty bound to add my own trajectory, which I often describe as a spiral, meaning that I continually return to the same points, but by way of a curve, seeking so far as possible to progress, to come ever closer to the source of Freudian thought while distancing myself from my older formulations (I have *Life and Death in Psychoanalysis* in particular in mind). One could even go so far as to imagine that these spirals of mine, like genetic spirals, curl around one another, but I will not entertain such speculations here.

(*At this point in my lectures for 1991–92 there followed a discussion on the Ptolemaic straying of Freudianism, which later served as an intro-duction to my book* La révolution copernicienne inachevée. Travaux 1967–1992.[8])

---

8 "Ponctuation: la révolution copernicienne inachevée, in *Révolution copernicienne*, pp. iii—xxxv. Eng. trans. by Luke Thurston: "The Unfinished Copernican Revolution," in Jean Laplanche, *Essays on Otherness*, ed. John Fletcher (London: Routledge, 1999 [hereafter *Essays on Otherness*]), pp. 52–83.

January 14, 1992

The major strayings

What I have proposed to call straying (there are several stray-ings, major and minor, all interconnected) is the result of Freud's retreat (an almost unavoidable retreat for which he should not be reproached) when confronted by the implications of the predominant role of the other in the constitution of—of what exactly? The subject? The individual? The person? Any of these terms no doubt, but each of them comes with heavy philosophical baggage. So let us just say: the constitution of the sexual human being.

Each of the major strayings may be clearly defined by what flows from it, by its post-Freudian progeny.

The first straying, which I will attempt to identify more pre-cisely and which is tied to a biologistic view of sexuality, has Melanie Klein and her school as its direct descendants.

The second, which I have already dealt with in part in discuss-ing the "Copernican revolution," is the self-centered reconstruction of the human being that dominates an entire school of psychology that claims allegiance in varying degrees to psychoanalysis.

The third straying consists in locating the structural at the heart of the unconscious, and its legacy can easily be discerned in the structuralism of Jacques Lacan.

There are other strayings, too, more or less subordinate to these major ones, among them phylogenesis and the notion of a primordial id, but all this classification is rather artificial—chiefly just a convenient way of presenting things.

Correcting for biologism does not mean rejecting biology

My theme for the moment is thus what might be called *the biologizing of the sexual drive*—a straying towards the biological. The expression is hazardous, however, and in need of clarification, for I have no wish to reject biology in the name of psychology, nor even in the name of the mental. To imply as much would come dangerously close to opposing mind to body, or psychology to biology, which is not my intention at all. It would also be a very risky option at a moment when a renewed offensive from the quarter of what is called the neurosciences or neurobiology has, as usual, taken psychoanalysis for one of its main targets. Psychoanalysis is continually being summoned to explain itself before the neurosciences. I cannot enter here into this debate with its many aspects; I have already done so on occasion, and I shall return to the question elsewhere, but not now.[9] Why should this accounting vis-à-vis the neurosciences be demanded of psychoanalysis in particular, rather than of any other interlocutor—with another of the human sciences, for example, or with aesthetics, history, logic, or political science? In any case, my present concern is connected only tangentially to the debate with the neurosciences, even if the existence of that debate argues for caution in our terminological choices.

What exactly do we mean by "the biologizing of the sexual drive"? Do we mean that sexuality is anchored in biology, and that each sexual excitation has a corresponding somatic aspect as well as a fantasy one? If so, there would obviously be no biologizing to challenge: even in the forms it assumes in humans, sexuality must be located somewhere in the body. The seduction theory, as adumbrated

---

9 See S. Jaffrin, "Repenser Freud: rencontre avec Jean Laplanche." Interview given to *Sciences Humaines* 10 (October 1991), pp. 32–35.

by Freud, certainly made the way forward difficult. How was one to conceive of the trace in the child's body of another person's perversion? Was there not a risk here of lapsing into philosophical idealism? Inasmuch as I have revived a general theory of seduction, the answers to these questions still need working out. I am thinking in particular of the recent research of Jacques André on the genesis of feminine sexuality, as cited last time (p. 7, note 6). André by no means closes the door to a vaginal sexuality founded on the conjunction of a sensitivity and a so-called "cloacal" excitation on the one hand and, on the other, adult fantasies of penetration. Be that as it may, we must firmly insist that the theory of seduction does not posit some kind of materialization of the mind in the body. On one side we have an organism that is a biological assembly but also a disposition of meaning (the infantile organism, oriented initially towards the more or less obscure goal of self-preservation); from the other side, the adult side, come mainly somatic messages inseparable from the gestural, mimetic, or auditory signifiers that deliver them.

Thus the issue is not the mind-body relationship but the articulation of sexual with self-preservative functioning, both being inextricably mental and somatic in character. The old problem of the mind-body split, as I have suggested elsewhere, if not solved in the Freudian perspective (and who would want to solve it?), is displaced onto another level, and that level is, precisely, the articulation embodied by "leaning-on" and seduction—a level which is not that of the introduction of the mental into the vital but rather that of the introduction of biopsychical sexuality into the equally biopsychical little human.

Abandonment of seduction: risk of a return to heredity

To speak of straying in connection with Freud's theory of sexuality obliges us to make clear the direction in which that theory was in danger of deviating. Let me quote here from the "letter of the equinox," in which Freud indicated two lines of thinking that, once the seduction hypothesis had been abandoned, were in his view reopened, and that in our view opened the way to straying: "It seems once again arguable that only later experiences give the impetus to fantasies which hark back to childhood, and with this the factor of a hereditary disposition regains a sphere of influence from which I had made it my task to dislodge it."[10]

These two paths down which it was now possible to travel, or to err, were on the one hand that of retroaction, of retroactive fantasy, and on the other of that of heredity. The first, the retroactive path, means treating sexuality simply in terms of adult imaginings projected back onto childhood. In point of fact Freud never embraced this notion: his commitment to the idea of infantile sexuality remained unshakable.

By contrast, the path of heredity or the innate, which I will define more clearly later, was always present in a lateral way for Freud, especially with respect to human sexuality. Before I come to *Three Essays on the Theory of Sexuality*, it is worth noting that in a letter to Fliess of November 14, 1897—thus not very long after the letter of the equinox—Freud was already describing a hereditary transmission of the successive stages of infantile sexuality (and notably the transition from anal to genital: a permanent Freudian paradigm).

Instinct and drive . . .

The danger of going astray after the abandonment of the seduction theory can be summed up in one word: instinct. The two phases of this danger may easily be associated with Freud's two theo-

10 Freud to Fliess, September 21, 1897. Jeffrey Moussaieff Masson, trans. and ed., *The Complete Letters of Sigmund Freud to Wilhelm Fliess 1887–1904* (Cambridge, Mass., and London: Harvard University Press, 1985) [hereafter *Letters to Fliess*], p. 265. [This is the letter in which Freud famously announced that "I no longer believe in my neurotica," thus signaling what was later considered his abandonment of the seduction theory. –Trans.]

ries of the drives: the first extends from *Three Essays on the Theory of Sexuality* to "Instincts and Their Vicissitudes" [or "Drives and Their Fates"], which is to say from 1905 to 1915; the second is initiated with the discovery of narcissism and completed by the theory of the "great" dualism of the life and death drives.[11]

Let us consider the first phase, from 1905 to 1915, focusing on the notion of instinct and the fact that Freud chose very early on to use the term *Trieb* despite the fact that *Instinkt* also exists in German. For Freud, *Trieb* accentuates the almost blind, demonic pressure for satisfaction rather than for any pre-established goal. The German language is peppered with doublets of this kind, where one of two words is of Latin origin—*Instinkt*, in this case, which comes from *instinguere*—and the other, here *Trieb*, is Germanic. *Instinkt* and *Trieb* are very similar in meaning, both connoting the idea of "inciting" or "pushing," but in such instances as this it falls to linguistic usage, and above all to the usage of an author, to create semantic distinctions.[12]

With respect to Freud there are two interpretations in this connection that must be rejected. The first is that of Lacan, who, in the context of his pro-"drive" radicalism (for which he should certainly not be rebuked), but also on account of his lack of familiarity with the entirety of Freud's work, simply denied that Freud "ever wrote" the word *Instinkt*.[13] In point of fact, the really interesting thing (and this by no means contradicts Lacan's train of thought) is to see just how the terms *Instinkt* and *Trieb* coexist within Freud's work.

---

11 I have dealt elsewhere with these two phases, first in Chapter 1 of *Life and Death* and later in *Problématiques III: la sublimation* (Paris: PUF, 1980). Between these two works my critical commentary was refined, and this process is continued here. For the second phase, see in particular Chapter 6 of *Problématiques IV: l'inconscient et le ça* (Paris: PUF, 1981), pp. 220–260.

12 See André Bourguignon, Pierre Cotet, Jean Laplanche and François Robert, *Traduire Freud* (Paris: PUF, 1989).

13 Jacques Lacan, *Écrits* (Paris: Le Seuil, 1966), p. 834; Eng. trans. by Bruce Fink, Héloïse Fink, and Russell Grigg: Écrits: *The First Complete Edition in English* (New York: Norton, 2005 [hereafter *Écrits* Complete in English]), p. 708 [translation rectified].

Lacan's error is ultimately no more than a lack of information. A much more seriously mistaken claim, underpinned by an interpretation at once banalizing and biologizing, maintains that when Freud uses the German word *Trieb*, it means the same thing as the French word *instinct*, and that therefore its French translation as *pulsion* is a kind of gratuitous complication, and an unjustified resort to a sort of Germanism.

... distinct terms for Freud ...

This distinction is clear and meaningful for Freud, who began using the word *Trieb* very early on—rarely at first but habitually after *Three Essays*—to designate the specific object of his thinking, namely sexuality, apropos of which he nevertheless continued to use *Instinkt*, along with the adjective *instinktuell* (instinctive or instinctual), though in a very different sense. In ordinary language, as in the countless texts where "instinctively" is used in the most natural way by Freud, the word refers to an almost automatic reaction, to a spontaneous response mechanism in a particular situation—contexts where the use of *Trieb* or *drive* would be completely inappropriate. For example: "Instinctively, I replied that (etc.)," or "By instinct, Lucky Luke drew his six-shooter." Who could fail to distinguish between the meaning there and the following: "possessed by a murderous impulse (or drive), the maniac brandished his revolver"? From dozens of instances in Freud, let me cite Lecture XXV of *Introductory Lectures on Psycho-Analysis* (1916-17), whose subject is anxiety and one of whose main ideas is that children in dangerous situations manifest little by way of anxiety or fear of an "instinctual" kind: "In all the situations which can later become determinants of phobias (on heights, on narrow bridges over water, on railway journeys, on ships) children exhibit no anxiety. . . . It would have been a very good thing if they had inherited more of such life-preserving instincts. . . . When in the end realistic anxiety is awakened in them, that is wholly the result of education; for they cannot be allowed to make the instructive experiences themselves."[14]

This text is interesting in its use of the term *Instinkt*, because it effectively defines it as a goal-directed (*zweckmässig*) and predetermined reaction received as an "inheritance"; it is interesting too in that it posits the almost complete absence, in humans, of instincts that would help them to escape danger automatically. The issue of anxiety comes up again in "Inhibitions, Symptoms and Anxiety" (1926), where its ultimate goal-directedness is again discussed and the word *Instinkt* used in certain well-defined contexts along with very specific expressions to evoke the possible instinctual character of anxiety: *Zweckmässigkeit*, assignment to a goal or goal-directedness; *zweckmässig*, goal-directed; *unzweckmässig*, non-goal-directed. The question being, is anxiety goal-directed from the outset as a way of averting danger, or is it rather a simple overwhelming wave with no particular purpose?

It is time to end this important digression on Freud's continual, conceptually circumscribed, and clearly defined use of *Instinkt* in texts where it would be quite impossible to understand anything were we to replace the term with its alleged synonym, *Trieb*.

But first let me attempt a definition of *Instinkt* in Freud's sense. The word denotes a behavioral mechanism with three features. First, it has a vital, biological purpose (*Zweckmässigkeit*)—for instance, the avoidance of danger. Behaviors of this kind that have been experimentally confirmed include the instinctual avoidance of the void by the young of cliff-dwelling birds. This purposefulness likewise characterizes the search for a particular habitat, or for a specific site suitable for mating or nesting during the great seasonal migrations.

A second feature is the invariability, in a single individual or

---

14 *Standard Edition* [hereafter SE] XVI, pp. 407–408. As early as the case history of Emmy von N. in *Studies on Hysteria* (1895), the two terms are clearly differentiated. In the first place, Freud evokes "the primary—or, one might say, the instinctive [*instinktiv*]—fear" provoked by certain animals (SE II, p. 87). Shortly thereafter, he calls the sexual drive (*Trieb*) the "most powerful of all" (SE II, p. 103).

in a given group, of a relatively fixed pattern (although the ethologists have shown that such instinctual schemata are susceptible to some variation).

Third and last, instinct has what may be called quite simply an innate character—that is, it is not acquired by the individual—but this without any presumption as to the manner of acquisition across a species; on this, as we know, debate is far from over. At all events, whether one is a neo-Darwinist or of some other persuasion, the mode of such acquisition is still a hypothetical matter awaiting discussion and verification, even if its hereditary rather than individual character is more easily confirmed.

These three characteristics—adaptiveness, invariability, inhereditedness—all of which are easily discernible in the principal texts in which Freud deals with *Instinkt*, are completely compatible with present-day accounts, even if those accounts include innumerable nuances, exceptions, and deviations. By way of example let me cite a little book by Gaston Viaud, *Les instincts*, which in particular summarizes the work of the ethologists, opening unhesitatingly, without raising any questions—and indeed perhaps there are none to be asked—with a grand typology of instincts, itself goal-defined: (1) instincts connected with preservation of the individual; (2) instincts connected with preservation of the species; and (3) instincts connected with preservation of the social group.[15] A similar framework may be said to obtain for Freud as well, however subject to question and revision: (1) self-preservation (i.e., preservation of the individual); (2) sexuality (the main problem here being that sexuality does not imply preservation of the species); and (3) maintenance of the social group, as witness Freud's discussion in *Group Psychology and the Analysis of the Ego* (1921) of the existence or not of a herd instinct (*Herdentrieb*).[16]

---

15 Paris: PUF, 1959.
16 SE XVIII, pp. 69–143, especially pp. 118ff.

. . . but always liable to confusion

In thus trying to situate the term *Instinkt* in Freud's think-ing, I also want to show how its use sometimes constitutes a kind of temptation, a kind of boundary, deviation, or straying. A straying of Freud's theory of sexuality in the direction of the instinctual is a perpetual possibility. It would perhaps be more accurate to speak of an instinctualizing rather than a biologizing of the sexual. It is fair to say that Freud struggled continually against this tendency: his rein-troduction of the instinctual factor into sexuality invariably followed a roundabout route—and this even in the most extreme instance.

Aristophanes' myth: its double interpretation by Freud

That "most extreme instance," namely the idea of the life and death drives, I shall come back to at the end of this course. But in the meantime, as a kind of preview of where I am headed, let me insert here a few thoughts on Freud's use of the celebrated myth that Plato has Aristophanes recount in the *Symposium*. Freud translates and glosses as follows: "'The original human nature was not like the present, but different. In the first place, the sexes were originally three in number, not two as they are now; there was man, woman, and the union of the two. . .' Everything about these primeval men was dou-ble: they had four hands and four feet, two faces, two privy parts, and so on. Eventually Zeus decided to cut these men in two, 'like a sorb-apple which is halved for pickling.' After the division had been made, 'the two parts of man, each desiring the other half, came together, and threw their arms about one another eager to grow into one.'"[17]

This myth is extremely clear in its attempt to account for sex-ual desire, which is said to arise from an original unity that has been lost and that we strive to reconstitute by finding what we very accu-

---

17 *Beyond the Pleasure Principle* (1920), SE XVIII, pp. 57–58.

rately describe as our other "half" (man + man or woman + woman in the case of homosexual love; man + woman for heterosexuality). Freud introduces the myth twice in his work, and offers two diametrically opposed commentaries on it.

Here, first of all, is what he writes at the beginning of *Three Essays on the Theory of Sexuality* (1905): "Popular opinion has quite definite ideas about the nature and characteristics of this sexual [drive]. It is generally understood to be absent in childhood, to set in at the time of puberty in connection with the process of coming to maturity and to be revealed in the manifestations of an irresistible attraction exercised by one sex upon the other; while its aim is presumed to be sexual union, or at all events actions leading in that direction. We have every reason to believe, however, that these views give a very false picture of the true situation. . . . The popular view of the sexual drive is beautifully reflected in the poetic fable which tells how the original human beings were cut up into two halves—man and woman—and how these are always striving to unite again in love."[18] In this instance, we see that Aristophanes' myth is cited because it backs up the popular view according to which sexuality is predetermined, and every Mr. Right finds his Miss Right according to an original harmony bound to be re-established. But Freud is quick to show his hand ("We have every reason to believe, however, that these views give a very false picture of the true situation [etc.]"), and throughout *Three Essays* he seeks to demolish this supposedly popular conception of sexuality as adaptive and harmonious.

But then, fifteen years on, in *Beyond the Pleasure Principle* (1920), after a lengthy exposition of his theory of the life and death drives, Freud argues that every drive is inhabited by a "compulsion to repeat" and strives to "return to an earlier state of things"; so far as the death drive is concerned, we know that the earlier state of things implies a return to

---

18 SE VII, pp. 135, 136. [Throughout this volume, where Strachey's *Standard Edition* translation is quoted, bracketed words (e.g., "sexual [drive]" above) indicate alterations reflecting Laplanche's preference. –Trans.]

inanimate matter, which puts an end to the energy imbalance created by the emergence of life. But what about the life instinct?

"If, therefore, we are not to abandon the hypothesis of death [drives], we must suppose them to be associated from the very first with life [drives]. But it must be admitted that in that case we shall be working upon an equation with two unknown quantities. Apart from this, science has so little to tell us about the origin of sexuality that we can liken the problem to a darkness into which not so much as a ray of a hypothesis has penetrated. In quite a different region, it is true, we *do* meet with such a hypothesis; but it is of so fantastical a kind—more myth than scientific explanation—that I should not venture to produce it here, were it not that it fulfills precisely the one condition whose fulfillment we desire. For it traces the origin of [a drive] to *a need to restore an earlier state of things*. What I have in mind is, of course, the theory which Plato put into the mouth of Aristophanes in the *Symposium*. . . ."[19]

There are thus two main occasions when Freud invokes Aristophanes: in 1905 he rejects the myth for being consistent with an opinion that he wishes to demolish, the idea of a predetermined sexuality; in 1920, to the contrary, he uses it to justify locating the origin of Eros or of the life drives (terms to which I will be returning) in a primal unity that might well be described as narcissistic.

Decoding the contradiction in Freud

Here we find ourselves in the most exemplary way faced with the problem of "interpreting Freud with Freud." One could say that Freud contradicts himself, but that does not get us very far, except to imply either that he does not know quite what he is saying or, alternatively, that he has forgotten what he said in *Three Essays* (which is indeed a possibility). Another view would be that Freud changed

---

19 *Beyond the Pleasure Principle*, SE XVIII, p. 57.

his mind about sexuality. If so, it was a 180-degree turn! After having argued that sexuality is not predetermined, the Freud of *Beyond the Pleasure Principle* seems to embrace the notion that everything is established in advance and that we strive only to return to what was present from the very beginning.[20] According to this reading, a quite superficial one, Freud turned his whole conception of sexuality upside down, and all his work on the distinction between drive and instinct thus went by the board. In a way this interpretation is now the received wisdom, even if some attempt is made to produce a sort of bastard synthesis of the two approaches. But who among Freudians would not throw up their hands in horror if offered the following proposition as the key to this puzzle: "Eros is not sexuality"? Of course, Eros is certainly *part* of sexuality. But when Freud began to postulate the kind of narcissistic Eros that tends to restore unity, what had happened to that erotic sexuality which for its part seeks anything but unity and is bound by no pre-established plan whatsoever? Either Freud had completely renounced everything he had ever said concerning *Lucifer amor*, and concerning the libido's destructiveness, or else that libido must be somewhere else, possibly in disguise, waiting to be unmasked.

When we read a text as violent as *Three Essays*, Freud's future "instinctual straying" from its theses is very hard to foresee. Michel Gribinski's excellent preface to the French translation published by Gallimard (he also mentions my *Life and Death in Psychoanalysis*) clearly underlines the emphatically polemical character of the work.[21] Even though much of the content of *Three Essays* was "well known," as Gribinski also points out—nor have critics failed to claim that Freud did nothing more than bring together elements from every point of the compass—the fact remains that the mixture was explosive.

---

20 In a poetic sense, of course. But the appeal to myth is too easy a way out: if a myth is correlated with an actual structure, even an atemporal one, this means that everything plays out in a sphere external to the manifestations of individual development.
21 Freud, *Trois essais sur la théorie sexuelle*, trans. Philippe Koeppel; preface by Michel Gribinski (Paris: Gallimard, Folio, 1992).

The dialectic of *Three Essays*

Beginning with Freud's introductory remarks, already cited apropos of Aristophanes, *Three Essays* may be looked upon as a kind of odyssey of instinct in three parts: instinct lost, in Parts I and II ("The Sexual Aberrations" and "Infantile Sexuality"), and, in Part III, instinct rediscovered—or perhaps rather, as I have suggested, instinct *mimed*, for what is eventually rediscovered is not precisely instinct but something that in humans resembles instinct without being truly instinctual.

"The Sexual Aberrations" is often described as a compilation, and Freud himself confirms this at the outset: "The information contained in this first essay is derived from the well-known writings of Krafft-Ebing, Moll, Moebius, Havelock Ellis [etc.]"[22] There is no search for originality in the matter of such aberrations, but an accumulation of arguments concerning their deviations relative to the *aim* (i.e., the process whereby pleasure is obtained); to the *object*; and, lastly, to the *source*, i.e., the sexual use of bodily zones other than those normally involved in coitus. All these deviations in the adult erode the idea of predetermination or goal-directedness, because the sole aim attributable to such acts, considered (rightly) to be sexual, cannot be related to a biological purpose but must rather imply a pure and simple search for pleasure.

"Infantile Sexuality" makes the same claim but with respect to the activity of the child. The theme is that sexuality exists in children, and that it is fundamentally perverse, perhaps even more perverse, or at any rate less regulated, less unified, than in adults. This is what Freud calls "polymorphous perversity." Here too much is made of the fact that all this has always been well known. But this is not to say that it was acknowledged; it is likewise true that the findings of Freud and the psychoanalysts in this regard probably never came as a surprise to "popular" views. One of the strongest pieces of evidence

---

22 *Three Essays on the Theory of Sexuality* [hereafter *Three Essays*], SE VII, p. 135n.

for the existence of infantile sexuality is the fact that it is forever being condemned, repressed, and denied by adults. This continues to be true today, in 1992, notwithstanding all the "sexual liberation" that has gone on.[23] If there is one kind of sexuality that continues to be condemned despite the modern liberal climate, it is surely the sexuality of children. Remarkably, however, even when its existence is accepted, at least in theory, it is usually placed under the rubric of genitality, or in other words ascribed to a precocious arousal of the genital organs. And as proof of this spontaneity, the occurrence of erections in the little boy, for instance, is continually cited—as though this was essentially what Freud had in mind. In point of fact, what Freud meant by infantile sexuality was only genital in the most contingent way; the epithet "polymorphous" applied not only to the type of activity but also to the zones excited in the child, which Freud thought multiple, and indeed ultimately to include the entire body.

As for the third part, "The Transformations of Puberty," it might be said to describe a return to instinct, or at least to something like instinct: a return in the first place to genitality and in the second to a sexual object, to the proverbial "person of the opposite sex"—in other words, an apparent return to the straight and narrow demands of instinct. It is true, however, that Freud has little to say about what he takes to be a "biological" goal, namely the rediscovered goal of procreation.

The introduction of goal-directedness
in later editions of *Three Essays*

It is difficult for an unprepared reader of *Three Essays* to grasp the subversive quality of this work, its deeply "perverse" character, and above all its emphasis on the absence of norms in human sexuality. This is because the book was revised by Freud many times. The first edi-

---

23 And despite all the brilliant paradoxes pointed up by the likes of Michel Foucault.

tion appeared in 1905, but Freud made lengthy additions in 1910, 1915, 1920, and 1924. All of these tended in the same direction, which was to deemphasize the aberrant nature of sexuality. Thirty or forty years ago, editions of the work made no mention at all of these successive changes, so that even leading psychoanalytical authors maintained that the notion of an anal stage or of narcissism had been part of Freudian theory as early as 1905. (Even the German *Gesammelte Werke* gave the 1924 edition of *Three Essays* without editorial commentary.) Today we have more critical editions explaining the additions by means of footnotes. Nevertheless, it would be of great help were one able to read the first version as it appeared in 1905 and thus truly get a sense of its original impact as well as of Freud's subsequent trajectory. For Freud's rewriting over the years constituted a sort of syncretic operation whereby his thought was deeply modified. To read the initial text, with all the later changes blacked out, would be to understand what a great hiatus, what a gulf, separates Part II from Part III, polymorphous perverse infantile sexuality from the reconfigurations of puberty. The definitive edition does introduce all of Freud's later innovations, but it merely interpolates them without providing any perspective. In particular, the second part is expanded to include what are called the "sexual organizations" or "infantile sexual stages," all of them strictly absent from the 1905 edition. The idea of an infantile sexuality already "organized" was formulated only later by Freud, in the wake of a series of papers based on his clinical work. Introduced in succession were the anal organization (the first great non-genital organization identified by Freud), the oral organization, which was not really a discovery in its own right but which took its place in the sequence after the anal organization, and, last and most important, what Freud called the infantile genital organization, based on the phallic/castrated dichotomy.[24]

Considering this interpolation of infantile sexual organizations, it is clear right away that the term "organization" suffices in

---

24 See my *Problématiques II: Castration et symbolisations* (Paris: PUF, 1980).

itself to introduce some idea of goal-directedness; what is much more, once the series is complete, what a great temptation it is to view this sequence of stages ranked chronologically—oral, anal, genital—as something closely resembling a predetermined and integrative development. And this view was indeed destined for great success thanks to one of Freud's chief disciples, Karl Abraham, who pushed this idea as far as it would go in what has been called "stageism."

From the moment this sequence is presented as predetermined, advancing toward a final stage referred to as objectality or genitality, and from the moment this ontogenetic sequence is presumed to reproduce a phylogenetic one, what I earlier called the "instinct lost" of Part I of *Three Essays* turns out to have been lost in appearance only. Infantile sexuality remains in the mists, but the road ahead leads it inevitably to adult sexuality, which conforms to "popular opinion." This kind of teleology has now been embraced by every brand of psychoanalytically inspired developmental psychology, but Abraham was the indisputable pioneer.

An essential observation: the notion of goal-directedness predominates here to the extent that the theory of sexual development claims to account for human development as a whole; only inasmuch as such pansexualism holds sway over the theory will there be an imperative need to describe a genesis of access (at once perceptual and sexual) to the object. On the other hand, and by virtue of a perfectly justified reversal, the pansexualism that strives to be all, to ignore and scorn any self-preservative development, inevitably degenerates into a purely relational theory. So let me finish today with the following proposition: the specificity of the sexual can manifest itself only when the existence of a non-sexual sphere is reaffirmed in some way, at least potentially. Next time I shall start out from this dualism of the self-preservative and the sexual.

January 21, 1992

Leaning-on: bibliographical references

I will be talking today about the concept of *Anlehnung* ("leaning-on"[25]), about the straying off-track to which this notion can lead, and about the indispensable correction of this wayward tendency.

Let me first mention and situate a number of works without discussing them in detail. In the first place, I have in mind the first edition of *Three Essays on the Theory of Sexuality* (1905), as augmented (and in a way undermined) by a short article of Freud's entitled "My Views on the Part Played by Sexuality in the Aetiology of the Neuroses" (1906).[26] Secondly, I refer to the writings of 1910–1912 in which Freud introduced the self-preservative drives along with a dualism between those drives (*Selbsterhaltungstriebe*) and the sexual ones (*Sexualtriebe*). There are several relevant texts here, among them "The Psycho-Analytic View of Psychogenic Disturbances of Vision" (1910),[27] which includes an account of leaning-on that was to be revisited in later editions of *Three Essays*. Third comes the very important discussion of masturbation, comprising two short texts by Freud ("Introduction"

---

25 [On the English translation of *Anlehnung*, for which James Strachey in the *Standard Edition* invented the term "anaclisis," see John Fletcher's introduction to *Essays on Otherness*, pp. 24–25. In his 1976 translation of *Life and Death*, Jeffrey Mehlman rendered the term as "propping." In choosing the term "leaning-on," the present translation follows the lead of more recent translators. –Trans.]
26 SE VII, pp. 269–279.
27 SE XI, pp. 211–214.

and "Concluding Remarks"[28]) and the minutes of eight sessions of the Vienna Psychoanalytical Society, each introduced by a member of the Society, held between November 22, 1911, and April 24, 1912 (this final date being the occasion of Freud's conclusion).[29] Fourth, and last, come "On Narcissism: An Introduction" (1914) and "[Drives] and Their Vicissitudes" (1915).[30]

The "invention" of the concept of *Anlehnung* by Laplanche and Pontalis . . .

So, what exactly is *Anlehnung*? A very long time ago now, J.-B. Pontalis and I decided to translate this term by the French word *étayage*, as suggested by a translator, now long forgotten, who chose it in order to save the notion from oblivion—more than oblivion, in fact, or perhaps rather from an "initial" oblivion, so to speak, for the idea had never really been "introduced," even by Freud.[31]

The concept of *Anlehnung* strives to express a particular basic articulation between two types of functioning and two modes of satisfaction. Between, on the one hand, a sexual functioning which in the child is precisely *not* a sexual function but which nevertheless foreshadows the biological function of sexuality, and, on the other, a self-preservative functioning, itself far more functional even if partly deficient in the young human.

For the basic definition of this term, allow me to direct you

---

28 "Contributions to a Discussion on Masturbation," SE XII, pp. 243–254.
29 *Minutes of the Vienna Psychoanalytical Society*, ed. Herman Nunberg and Ernst Federn, trans. Margarete Nunberg, vols. III and IV (New York: International Universities Press, 1974, 1975).
30 SE XIV, pp. 69–102 and pp. 111–140 respectively.
31 I have been asked, once again just recently, how I feel about the use of *étayage* by René Kaës. Whatever the merits of this author's work, I find it regrettable and harmful that he should borrow this important and difficult term, so carefully defined in my and J.-B. Pontalis's *Vocabulaire de la psychanalyse*, to express ideas whose link to the Freudian notion is anything but obvious. It is not as though other words were not available.

to the various relevant articles of *Vocabulaire de la psychanalyse / The Language of Psycho-Analysis*, which cover the question thoroughly.[32] Suffice it here to cite one particularly explicit passage from Freud: "The sexual [drives] find their first objects by [leaning-on what is valued] by the ego-[drives], precisely in the way in which the first sexual satisfactions are experienced [leaning-on] the bodily functions necessary for the preservation of life."[33] Two words are notable in this passage: first, "value," as used later by others, by the ethologists, and in their wake by Daniel Lagache, who laid much stress on the idea that the object of self-preservation is found in the environment, as a "food value"; secondly, the notion of bodily *function*, a serious competitor to that of *drive*—and indeed perhaps more apt in the case of self-preservation.

... by putting Freud to the "test of translation"

Is *Anlehnung*, or leaning-on, a "Freudian concept"? I have discussed this with François Robert, my collaborator in charge of terminological questions for the translation into French of Freud's complete works.[34] To ask the question is to suggest the possibility of distinguishing in Freudian thought between different levels of conceptualization: between concepts, quasi-concepts, para-concepts, and so on. What we have in this case may be described as a concept never identified as such by Freud, who never wrote—and would never have dreamt of writing—an article on *Anlehnung*. Furthermore, for many years it had no specific entry in indexes, even in those to German editions of Freud's works. The idea was identified in the main

---

32 Jean Laplanche and J.-B. Pontalis, *Vocabulaire de la psychanalyse* (Paris: PUF, 1967), esp. s.v. "Étayage." Eng. trans. by Donald Nicholson-Smith: *The Language of Psycho-Analysis* (London: Hogarth Press / Institute of Psycho-Analysis, 1973; New York: Norton, 1974), esp. s.v. "Anaclisis; Anaclitic (or Attachment)."
33 "On the Universal Tendency to Debasement in the Sphere of Love," SE XI, pp. 180–181.
34 *Oeuvres complètes de Freud / Psychanalyse* (Paris: PUF, 21 vols., 1988–).

by translators, alerted by the recurrence of the same word or the same notion. This is what, following Antoine Berman, I refer to as the "test of the foreign"[35]: when a thought undergoes such a test of translation, constants are exposed, coalescing tendencies, that may not have been evident either to Freud himself or to readers of his German text. In more than one way the term *Anlehnung* is quite similar to *Nachträglichkeit*, which also belongs to the category of "implicit concepts" or "para-concepts." While *Nachträglichkeit—après-coup*, or "afterwardsness"—was essentially identified by Lacan, *Anlehnung* was first brought to the fore by Pontalis and myself.[36]

Concepts like these have a peculiar status. They offer a very rich lode for post-Freudian prospecting, but their potential must in large measure be teased out, for the simple reason that Freud himself did not exploit it, leaving their role, as pivotal as it might be, ill-defined and untheorized—central, yet only implicit. Their value is thus something that we, as post-Freudians, must bestow on them. Two years ago [in 1989–90], I gave a course on the *après-coup* effect in the development of the concept of *après-coup*[37]; similarly, my present subject might be described as the après-coup of leaning-on. In addition, these two concepts share a curious fate: the very moment at which they were about to crystallize, just as Freud became aware of his systematic use of them, was also the moment they came under threat of impoverishment. They were fully conceptualized just as they went into decline. Consider the fate of *Nachträglichkeit*. The adjective *nachträglich* made its appearance in Freud's works during the period of great innovation enshrined in the correspondence with Wilhelm Fliess, the period of the seduction theory; later on, the

---

35 See Antoine Berman, *L'épreuve de l'étranger. Culture et traduction dans l'Allemagne romantique: Herder, Goethe, Schlegel, Novalis, Humboldt, Schleiermacher, Hölderlin* (Paris: Gallimard, 1984). Eng. trans. by Stefan Heyvaert: *The Foreign: Culture and Translation in Romantic Germany* (Albany, NY: SUNY Press, 1992).

36 Some people have attributed the development of the concept of *Anlehnung* to Lacan, but the notion is actually quite foreign to him.

37 Transcribed as *Problématiques VI: L'après-coup.* (Paris: PUF, 2006).

term *Nachträglichkeit* was introduced, sealing the transformation of the adjective into a substantive—and hence into a concept. But this promotion to the dignity of a concept occurred just a few weeks *after* Freud had abandoned the seduction theory, as he wrote Fliess, and with it *Nachträglichkeit's* rich potential, as from now on he would give the concept a mechanistic sense and eliminate any connotation of a reversal of the arrow of time.[38] The idea of *après-coup* as used by Freud in this letter was no longer anything more than a ticking time bomb within the subject. Any suggestion of a possible retroactive effect—any notion of an antero-posterior action, so to speak, which is what made the concept so rich—was gone: it was thus exactly at the time when *Nachträglichkeit* was deprived of its foundation, namely the seduction theory, that the term was suddenly substantivized.[39]

Self-preservation/sexuality: a dualism, not a parallelism

Much the same sort of thing may be said about *Anlehnung*. Consider the state of affairs in 1905. A fog covers the origins of sexuality. The idea of a "self-preservative drive" is nowhere to be found; self-preservation is generally categorized as a function or need, never as a drive. The relationship between sexual drive and self-preservation is likewise being sought, and this, in the first edition of *Three Essays*, by means of different words, notably *Vergesellschaftung*, or "association." The term *Anlehnung* occurs but once in this work, where it serves to denote the leaning of anal sexuality on the function of excretion.

One part of my thesis is that it was just when leaning-on was about to be properly conceptualized in the years 1910–1912 that it ran the risk of going astray: this was the moment when self-preservation

---

38 Freud to Fliess, November 14, 1897, *Letters to Fliess*, pp. 278–282.
39 All this is clearly explained in *Problématiques VI: L'après-coup*. See also "Notes on Afterwardsness," in *Essays on Otherness*, pp. 260–265.

was said by Freud to be a drive *parallel* to sexuality, and made up of the same components.

Self-preservation would now be modeled on sexuality, and by a reciprocal process this would alter the conception of the sexual drive. Defining a function in terms of a drive ran the risk of reducing the drive to the status of a function—in other words, of recharacterizing sexuality in a purely functionalist way.

Hence the paradoxical position of those who, like me, interpret a latent concept of this sort; such an interpreter conceptualizes what Freud never conceptualized, demonstrates how fruitful the result can be, and proposes a way out—a rescue mission—for a significant problem in the work in question; but he must also show how this rescue itself can be caught up in what I call straying, how it can itself take that wayward path.

This straying-away of *Anlehnung* (and within *Anlehnung*) is what I want to expand on here, although I concluded a good while ago—in *Problématiques III*, devoted to sublimation—that "the seduction theory alone explains the true nature of leaning-on."[40]

The four Freudian aspects of the drive

At this point we are obliged to recall Freud's four dimensions or aspects of the drive in their seeming simplicity, but also in their vast ambiguity, as uncovered little by little. These dimensions are the source (*Quelle*), the aim (*Ziel*), the object (*Objekt*), and the pressure (*Drang*) of the drive. Here I refer you to the respective entries in *The Language of Psycho-Analysis* and to relevant portions of *Life and Death in Psychoanalysis*[41] and *Problématiques III*.[42]

---

40 *Problématiques III: La sublimation* (Paris: PUF, 1980), p. 69.
41 *Life and Death*, pp. 8–14.
42 *Problématiques III*, pp. 21–31. The only detail I have to add concerns the distinction that should be drawn between what Freud calls *Ziel*, or aim, and the problematic *Zweck*, or goal. In the case of *Ziel*, what is at issue is not an intention but rather a

On the question of human sexuality, a careful examination of these four notions, with their internal contradictions, leads to the same conclusion as that drawn from the observations brought together in *Three Essays*.

In the sexual drive, every aspect is variable. The *object* is contingent, liable to any number of substitutions; Freud noted that any object may be replaced by any other. The *aim* is susceptible to exchange, modification, and inhibition. And *sources* are interconnected, and prone to stand in for one another. On this view, object, aim, and source, in the case of the sexual drive, are all ultimately evanescent. This brings to mind "Jeannot's knife," all of whose parts had been replaced. Or perhaps the ship of Theseus as described by Plutarch. At the time when Plutarch was writing his *Parallel Lives*, the boat in which Theseus had sailed centuries before on his way to slaying the Minotaur in Crete was still on display in Athens. Since this genuine historical relic was of course made of wood, over the years, as one piece after another rotted, every single plank had been changed. According to Plutarch, the boat thus became an object that the philosophers used as an example: if every part has been replaced, they wondered, could this still be called "the ship of Theseus"?

The drive is much like the ship of Theseus. What remains of it? Nothing, in the end, except *pressure*—that *Drang* which, semantically speaking, is synonymous with *Trieb*. This is, I believe, what Lacan meant to point out when he mused that the word *dérive* (drift)

form of behavior, a sequence involving consummation and satisfaction. As for *Zweck* and *Zweckmässigkeit* (see p. 17 above), they refer to the teleology of behavior. It is notable that Freud, as opposed as he was at the outset to a teleological view of drives, sometimes gave way on the matter, as he did with respect to infantile masturbation, where he at first acknowledged "nature's purpose of establishing the future primacy" of the genital zone; he then accepted the criticism of his disciple Rudolph Reitler and withdrew this phrase in editions of *Three Essays* after 1910 (SE VII, p. 188 n. 1). But in 1920, after the introduction of the life and death drives, he accepted the inevitability, still doubtful in 1915 (ibid., p. 156, n. 1), of taking a teleological view in biology (ibid., p. 184 n. 2).

might serve as an alternative to *pulsion* as the French translation of *Trieb*. No translator, of course, not even a Lacanian one, would dare render the title of Freud's well-known text as "Dérives et destins de dérives" (Drifts and Their Vicissitudes), but Lacan's play on words, based on the similarity between the English *drive* and the French *dérive*, does suggest the idea that the drive is adrift or, in other words, that *Trieb* indicates no set course.[43] Of endogenous origin, it signals nothing save perhaps the need to get rid of it as quickly as possible. Only pressure remains, and pressure is blind.

---

43 Jacques Lacan, *Écrits* (Paris: Seuil, 1966), p. 803; Écrits *Complete in English*, p. 680.

January 28, 1992

Source, aim, pressure, object. Now that we have recalled these four notions, which are not so simple but which serve Freud—and us—as rough points of reference, let me come to our main topic, namely *Anlehnung*, or leaning-on. This concept addresses a problem of origins that arises as an explicitly temporal one. There is no justification for rejecting questions of time and chronology by appealing to some sort of atemporality. The task is to account for the very first appearance of sexuality or, in other words, for *infantile* sexuality.

Infantile sexuality: why question its origins if it does not exist?

This raises the preliminary question of why one would try to account for something that is nonexistent. Debate over this has not yet ended, and the ways infantile sexuality is denied are legion. It may be denied flatly, or explicitly, or dismissed as aberrant, as pathological, based solely on observation of a few exceptional cases. It may be contested on another level too, as a phenomenon of a biological kind and of endogenous origin—though this does not amount to denying its existence. Lastly, it may be denied in a subtler but more dangerous manner within the psychoanalytic movement itself by being desexualized, swamped by something else so that it loses its specifically sexual character. Such efforts are widespread and persistent even today. What Freud referred to as Jung's views (while acknowledging his temporary alignment with them) did exactly that, but making libido or Eros into everything comes down to making it into nothing. It completely avoids the real problem, which is to define and situate infantile sexuality. Other strategies prevail today, however, like the tendency to dilute sexuality into what is known as object relations, with the term "sexual" relegated utterly to a secondary status except for its application to the strictly genital—precisely what Freud did not intend.

In the case of infantile sexuality we are concerned with something very specific that we call a broadened sexuality—broadened, that is, to include the pregenital; and perhaps we should call it *extra-*genital sexuality to guard against any chronological assumptions with regard to what may follow the pregenital within the broad category of sexuality, assumptions such as the all-too-familiar sequence of stages: oral, anal, urethral, etc. In the last reckoning, anything at all may become sexual in the functioning of the human being.

Proof, definition, and foundation are inseparable

Infantile sexuality poses a seemingly two-part problem of proof and definition. But this is where we need to adopt a somewhat dialectical approach, for the problem is not really twofold in that the proof of sexuality and of its generalization derives the actual essence (and hence the definition) from the existence of what is to be proved. In other words, it is not a matter of (1) I define x as sexual and (2) I show you that x actually exists. Rather, I show you that x exists and precisely thereby *produce* a different idea, an idea not unconnected to the original one, to the common view, but which indeed derives from it.

In an article written in 1971, "The Derivation of Psychoanalytic Entities," I tried to show apropos of many psychoanalytic concepts that their definition, their genesis, entails their existence.[44] To return

---

44 "Dérivation des entités psychanalytiques," in *Hommage à Jean Hyppolite* (Paris: PUF, 1971), pp. 195–215. Reprinted in *Révolution copernicienne*, pp. 106–123. Eng. trans. by Jeffrey Mehlman: "The Derivation of Psychoanalytic Entities," Appendix to *Life and Death in Psychoanalysis*, pp. 127–139.

to much simpler questions, all derivation follows universal and long-recognized paths, classified as early as the sixteenth century, the paths of the association of ideas and, I would add, the linking of things or entities. These principles are three and three only: resemblance, contiguity, and opposition.

In Lecture XX of *Introductory Lectures on Psycho-Analysis*,[45] as well as in *Three Essays*, these three modalities of the proof and simultaneous derivation of infantile sexuality may all be observed in operation.

Resemblance. Freud has this operate on the plane of orgasm, arguing that there are phenomena on levels other than the genital where something resembling the orgasmic event in adults is to be observed. Another resemblance—more probative in my view—is that between numerous pleasurable infantile activities and practices among perverts that are universally deemed sexual in nature.

Contiguity or continuity. The argument from contiguity is generally defended by reference to the forms of forepleasure that accompany or precede the properly genital act in adults and involve many zones and processes other than genital ones. So-called forepleasure (*Vorlust*) is at once *contiguous* to the genital act, which it prepares for, and *similar* to infantile sexuality.

This interplay between resemblance and contiguity—which I call metabolism or symbolization—gives rise to a *derivation* (Lacan uses the word *dérive*, or drift) with respect both to proof and to existence. It would be rash indeed to claim either that such a proof is extrinsic or that it has not brought the *thing itself* into being.

Lastly, there is the argument from *opposition*. This is not quite the same as an argument from the contrary, but it is a decidedly important test, and a specifically psychoanalytic one. Freud brings it up at the very beginning of the second part of *Three Essays*, in the section entitled "Neglect of the Infantile Factor." This proof is based on the

---

45 SE XVI, pp. 303–319.

systematic reluctance of scientific authors to mention infantile sexuality. A proof, then, based on repression. The specialists here merely represent adults in general, who repress their own childhood sexuality and condemn any signs of such sexuality in the outside world. Such phenomena would not be denounced with the same fervor as that directed at adult sexual perversions were they not condemned *internally* before being condemned outwardly.

You will have noticed that these tests imply a new definition, which in turn (and this is my own addition) implies *the need for a new foundation.*

Freud's threefold definition of infantile sexuality is worth quoting in full: "At its origin, it [leans on] one of the vital somatic functions; it has as yet no sexual object, and is thus auto-erotic; and its sexual aim is dominated by an erotogenic zone."[46]

All aspects of the drive are present here except for pressure: aim, object, source (the erotogenic zone). But notice the predominance given to leaning-on: it was introduced into this passage by Freud only *après-coup*, so to speak, in 1915, but it is placed at the beginning of the definition, as if in a way the key—the glimpsed key—to infantile sexuality.

Just as seduction, as I am forever repeating, may be considered the key to leaning-on, so leaning-on itself may be considered the belatedly revealed key to autoerotism and the erotogenic zones. The first element, leaning-on, is dynamic: it defines while at the same time creating, whereas the second and third present problems concerning the essence of the matter that are liable to bog the discussion down. The problem raised by the third assertion, with the *aim* dominated by a somatic zone, is that of the *biological*; as to the second, concerning autoerotism, the problem of the presence or absence of the *object* opens up the whole issue of the fantasy object.

Let me say a few words about these two problems to clarify

---

46 SE VII, pp. 182–183.

what is at stake here. Naturally we shall get back to them, and expand on them, in our discussion of leaning-on.

The problematic relationship of aim to source

First consider the issue of the biological as raised by the third phrase in Freud's definition according to which "its sexual aim is dominated by an erotogenic zone." This proposition has two closely related implications: first the primacy of the "source" and secondly the need to discuss "organ-pleasure."

Once one says that the aim—the accomplished action—is under the sway (*unter der Herrschaft*) of the source, and that the source is by definition some erotogenic zone, this immediately implies a great impoverishment of the aim: in the first place, the poor erotogenic zone, be it the lips, the anus, or the penis, can have no aim but detumescence or something akin to it; moreover, this position provokes the temptation—and repeated attempts—to biologize the source as well, which is to say to attribute a predilection for this or that zone (the reason this or that zone is chosen), and ultimately to a process that is itself physiological, as for instance the distribution of sexual hormones. Any such prioritizing assignment of certain hormones to sites not confined to genital ones, and including for instance various erotogenic zones, would, of course, have to be demonstrated.

This is where the current arguments of the defenders of a biological infantile sexuality are perfectly self-contradictory: by basing the notion of infantile sexuality on specific facts, such as erections in male infants, they simply brush aside what Freud was concerned with, namely a broadened conception of that sexuality as predominantly extragenital. Those arguments also fail to address the question of the little girl's sexuality—to which Freud paid very close attention—by concentrating exclusively on genital excitement in little boys.

What is more, this idea of a tight dependence of the aim upon a somatic zone is really viable only for a few component drives, a few specific mucous membranes invariably used as references, whereas for other erotic pleasures it is obvious that the notion of detumescence or tumescence is beyond our comprehension. Take, for example, what Freud calls the drive to look (*Schautrieb*). It is hardly a detumescence of the eye—save perhaps in the most metaphorical sense—that the voyeur seeks. Clearly this notion of a sort of secretion of sexuality by a somatic source or erotogenic zone does not get us very far.

A problematic object relationship: the fantasy object

I come now to the other problem, that of autoerotism defined as without an object: "Infantile sexuality has as yet no sexual object, and is thus auto-erotic." The main issue resides in this claim: does sexuality lack a real object but have a fantasy one, or does it have no object at all? It must be acknowledged that when Pontalis and I wrote in the entry on autoerotism in *The Language of Psycho-Analysis*, and when I reiterated, in what I have since written about leaning-on, that autoerotism is bound to fantasy, we were talking about what we would like Freud to have said, though he did not. The fact is that for Freud autoerotism means "completely without an object," whether external to one's own body or fantasized: lacking any external object, even an object that is "external" in fantasy.

There is nevertheless an evolution in Freud's thinking that is connected to the way he gradually pushes sexuality further and further back relative to age. This rollback of sexuality was paralleled by a rollback of the time of fantasy's emergence. In 1905 *Three Essays* rather sharply contrasted an entire childhood with no object, and thus "auto-erotic," and a puberty that entailed discovery of the object. And in a contemporary article, "My Views on the Part Played by Sexuality in the Aetiology of the Neuroses," which rounded out and underscored certain biologizing tendencies of *Three Essays*, fantasies were said to be generated in the main at puberty and projected backwards.[47]

Then came the aforementioned discussions of masturbation by the Vienna Psychoanalytical Society in 1911–1912, which inevitably touched on the definition of autoerotism, and which were recorded in the Society's *Minutes*.[48]

An initial discussion of masturbation took place in 1910, but the debate was so contradictory that it was abandoned after two or three sessions. The subject was taken up once more in 1911–1912 and continued step by step over eight meetings, roughly every two weeks. Let me cite a few interventions concerning the problem of autoerotism.

Ernst Federn asked the question "whether a sexual fantasy is linked with every sort of masturbating (*ob mit jeder Onanie eine sexuelle Phantasie verknüpft sei*)."[49] Note the stress on the word *sexuelle* in the original.

The question was a good one, and Wilhelm Stekel responded to it in precise fashion at the next meeting: "Stekel characterizes as masturbation any sexual activity that is performed without the cooperation of another person and would regard it as being, quite apart from the fantasies, autoerotic."[50] In all instances, with or without fantasy, so long as no real outside person was present, autoerotism was involved.

Freud for his part had earlier expressed an opposing view quite forcefully: "Freud states that as a rule we characterize as 'autoerotic' only the first two years of life, the masturbation of the subsequent period with fantasies about other persons is no longer purely 'autoerotic.'"[51] In other words, once there was an outside object, even in fantasy, autoerotism no longer really existed.

---

47 1906 [1905]. SE VII, p. 274.
48 Vols III and IV. See p. 28, n. 29 above.
49 Ibid., vol. IV, p. 22.
50 Ibid., p. 36.
51 Ibid., p. 25.

Elsewhere in these discussions Freud offered more detail: three main periods of masturbatory activity should be clearly distinguished: from birth to two years old, from three to five, and puberty. In 1905 Freud thought that fantasy arises only with puberty. In these discussions he thus conceded that it is active earlier, between the ages of three and five, but he maintained that the real autoerotic period is the very first, when no fantasy is present.

To continue with my assemblage of citations, let me mention Gaston Rosenstein's remark that "the question about fantasies is connected with (*zusammenhängt*) the question of autoerotism; if the fantasies are related to another person, masturbation is no longer purely autoerotic." Thus Rosenstein is in complete agreement with Freud's point of view: from the moment a fantasy involves another person, even if the act is performed alone, one should speak of masturbation but not of autoerotism. Rosenstein goes on: "In his conception of unconscious fantasies, Federn [who had said that unconscious fantasies might occur between birth and two years of age] sees in the unconscious not merely the repressed but also the innate component part of the psyche."[52]

The door is thus opened to the presence of fantasies between birth and the age of two—fantasies that are not internalizations by the subject of relationships in the outside world but rather of internal origin. One thinks immediately of the unrepressed hereditary id and of what that was destined to become in Freud later on. Federn opened a door, one might say, that the Kleinians went through without ever coming back out when they espoused the idea of fantasies with no external origin, but there from the start.

Let us take another look at Susan Isaacs's "The Nature and Function of Phantasy," from 1948.[53] A classic. Unlike the Freud of 1901–1915, Isaacs considers fantasy to be present from the beginning

---

52 Ibid., pp. 23–24.
53 *International Journal of Psychoanalysis* 29 (1948), pp. 73–97; reprinted in Melanie Klein et al., *Developments in Psycho-Analysis* (London: Hogarth Press, 1950).

as unconscious fantasy. She means unconscious fantasies of endogenous origin. It has had to be said over and over again, but it really is like this among Kleinians: the entire fantasy life of the child is present from the outset, and this *internally*, even though it is able to take advantage of *external* factors. And to understand this Kleinian view of fantasy life the operation of the drive must be conceived of as a process with two aspects: a purely physiological aspect and an unconscious psychic aspect in a recto-verso relationship.[54] This is concordant with a whole line of thinking within Freudianism that views the unconscious as preceding the rise of consciousness, thus giving priority to a sort of atavistic unconscious present from the outset.

I shall be returning at the end of this course to the question of Kleinianism, which constitutes the furthermost point reached by the endogenous straying that is my theme.

---

54 Let me digress for a moment and mention a recent book which has not received enough attention, Gérard Mendel's *La psychanalyse revisitée* (Paris: La Découverte, 1988). It is easy to agree with Mendel on a whole section of his reasoning, especially two theses that he himself was surprised to find coincided precisely with my views, namely the rejection of any biological infantile sexuality and the rejection of the inheritance of archaic fantasies—the famous primal fantasies. Certain convergences of this sort have also been pointed out in an article by Amine A. Azar, "La malédiction des pharaons pèse-t-elle sur les pyschanalystes?" (Has the Curse of the Pharaohs Fallen on the Psychoanalysts?), *L'Évolution psychiatrique* 56 (1991), no. 1, pp. 177–187.

February 4, 1992

Leaning-on: the dihedron

I offered different diagrams of leaning-on in Volumes III and IV of *Problématiques*.[55] The simplest representation is that of a dihedron, which is to say the intersection of two planes, that of self-preservation and that of sexuality. Leaning-on occurs along the line of intersection:

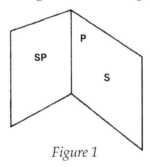

Figure 1

A more dynamic model is that of two arrows representing the two "drive impulses" (*Triebregungen*):

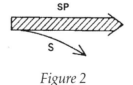

Figure 2

---

55 *Problématiques III: La sublimation* (Paris: PUF, 1980), esp. pp. 33ff; *Problématiques IV: L'inconscient et le ça* (Paris: PUF, 1982), Eng. trans. by Luke Thurston: *The Unconscious and the Id* (London: Rebus Press, 1999).

Let me first quote the pivotal passage from *Three Essays*. I make no comments on it here, for I have often done so elsewhere: "it is clear that the behavior of a child who indulges in thumb-sucking is determined by a search for some pleasure which has already been experienced and is now remembered. In the simplest case he proceeds to find this satisfaction by sucking rhythmically at some part of the skin or mucous membrane. It is also easy to guess the occasions on which the child had his first experiences of the pleasure which he is now striving to renew. It was the child's first and most vital activity, his sucking at his mother's breast, or at substitutes for it, that must have familiarized him with this pleasure. The child's lips, in our view, behave like an erotogenic zone, and no doubt stimulation by the warm flow of milk is the cause of the pleasurable sensation. The satisfaction of the erotogenic zone is associated, in the first instance, with the satisfaction of the need for nourishment. To begin with, sexual activity [leans on] functions serving the purpose of self-preservation and does not become independent of them until later.[56] No one who has seen a baby sinking back satiated from the breast and falling asleep with flushed cheeks and a blissful smile can escape the reflection that this picture persists as a prototype of the expression of sexual satisfaction in later life. The need for repeating the sexual satisfaction now becomes detached from the need for taking nourishment—a separation which becomes inevitable when the teeth appear and food is no longer taken in only by sucking, but is also chewed up."[57]

Three conceptions of leaning-on

How then are we understand the concept of leaning-on? Popular wisdom says that only the rich get loans. But Freud's notion of leaning-on may be said to have been enriched even though it is

56 This sentence, which places the whole passage a posteriori under the banner of *Anlehnung*/leaning-on, was added in 1915.
57 SE VII, pp. 181–182.

poorer in terms of its explicitness than one might wish; and at times one is indeed tempted to take back what has been loaned. To keep things simple, let me say that there are three possible interpretations of the articulation between self-preservation and sexuality: (1) a poor, parallelist interpretation; (2) an interpretation that is rich in the sense that it encompasses an emergence, but contradictory, so that its dialectic opens the door to (3) an inverted interpretation of leaning-on.

The poor, parallelist conception of leaning-on

The poor interpretation of leaning-on is founded on what is admittedly a strictly literal reading of Freud. There are very few mentions of leaning-on in Freud's work: in the passage just quoted from *Three Essays*, in the later additions to that book, and one reference in "[Drives] and Their Vicissitudes" (1915).[58] As for Freud's article on narcissism, which I will be coming back to later, it takes leaning-on as a given but does not describe it. This "poor" interpretation assumes a kind of genetic parallelism between the two types of drives, a parallel that, as I pointed out earlier, is quite dubious even as a descriptive analogy, since it is by no means certain that the term "drive" is apt for designating both self-preservation and sexuality. According to this model, neither of these processes would have much impact on the other, except with respect to the emergence of sexuality, or in other words at the level of the "source." The self-preservative function—nourishment in this case—is seen as the *occasion* of a stimulation of the erotogenic zone, which in this instance is the lips. ("It is . . . easy to guess the *occasions* on which the child had his first experiences of the pleasure which he is now striving to renew.") Such stimulation is destined to be repeated in an endogenous mode. This implies that there is a kind of disconnect at the source, between the source of self-preservation (hardly the lips: how could the lips be described as the

---

58 SE XIX, p. 126.

source of hunger?), which is to say the somatic process at the root of hunger, and a sexual source identified by Freud as the mucous membrane of the lips.

As for the *aim*, what are we told here? Nothing concrete, nothing really specific. The aim of the self-preservative drive is ingestion in the case of nourishment, excretion in the case of the excretory zones. No such aim can be found in autoerotic activity: "The source of [a drive] is a process of excitation occurring in an organ and the immediate aim of the [drive] lies in the removal of this organic stimulus."[59] Here we have the notion of "organ-pleasure": should there be tension in the lips, the point is to reduce it; should a mucous membrane be excited, it will be similarly excited whatever the direction of the stimulus, in or out, so that there is no direct relationship of derivation between the fulfilling alimentary act (or the aim) and the fulfilling sexual act (likewise the aim).

So in place of my earlier diagrams (Figures 1 and 2) we get the following:

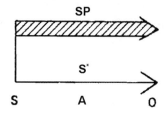

Figure 3

With respect to the *object*, things are contradictory. There is naturally no denying that self-preservation can point the way in the search for a sexual object (the parallelism represented in Figure 3), but for Freud the specificity of sexuality, the moment I describe in *Life and Death in Psychoanalysis* as the reflexive or "auto" moment of

---

59 SE VII, p. 168.

autoerotism,[60] involves no fantasy, so that there can be no relationship of *symbolization* between one object and another: it is simply that
one object is *replaced* by another within the body. The thumb being
"sucked" replaces nourishment, but in a completely mechanical and
non-signifying way.

This parallelism is destructive from every standpoint. It dam-
ages the conception of self-preservation and its complex mechanisms.
The fact is that Freud had scant interest in alimentary needs, which
originate not in the lips nor even in the stomach, but rather in a whole
set of highly complicated homeostatic regulatory processes. Similarly,
the source of excretion, of defecation, obviously does not lie in the
anus per se, but in mechanisms, perhaps somewhat less complex than
alimentary ones, that are well described in the physiology of intesti-
nal peristalsis.

The parallelist view also impoverishes the concept of sexuality and the issue of its source by explaining it on the model of sucking:
if sexuality were reducible to organ-pleasure, it would suffice to
assign different measures of sex hormone to different so-called erotogenic zones and other parts of the body—which I defy anyone to do.
This is not to say that no bodily zones are more sensitive than others,
but simply that the realm of potential sensitivity must be extended
to the entire skin surface, and even to more complex mechanisms,
anchored in the body but more complex, such as vision or muscular
activity, which Freud invoked in connection with "indirect sources"
of sexuality.[61]

Thus the parallelist approach, along with "[Drives] and Their
Vicissitudes" in general, is a kind of middling point of view that fails
to give a good account of self-preservation, or of sexuality, or of the
relationship between the two.

---

60 *Life and Death*, p. 88.
61 See ibid., pp. 21–22 and SE XVI, pp. 204–205.

Interpretation using the notion of emergence

A second type of interpretation preserves the notion of leaning-on by treating it as a kind of *emergence*. The visual representation here is the diagram (Figure 2, p. 45 above) with the self-preservation arrow and the second arrow (sexuality) gradually peeling off after having moved in parallel for a time. This is explained in *The Language of Psycho-Analysis* (s.v. "Anaclisis"), where the concept of leaning-on was first isolated, and in *Life and Death in Psychoanalysis*.

This view of leaning-on envisages not only support but also simultaneous distancing and borrowing. In other words, neither of the drives operates solely on its own account. Schematically speaking, leaning-on has two phases: first a functioning in tandem, then a distancing and divergence. Elsewhere Freud says as much explicitly: at first sexuality obtains satisfaction at the same time as feeding; then it splits off to become autoerotic. Thus, the emergence of autoerotism means a sharp change of direction—not a founding moment but a moment of becoming. I have often stressed the flattening out that occurred in Freud's views once he embraced the idea of autoerotism as the initial state of the life of the human being rather than as a secondary phase.

Conjunction, then, followed by an emergence based on a disconnection: a sort of metabolization or symbolization consonant with the general principles of association, which, I repeat, are inescapable not only in thought but also within the living being: specifically, the principles of contiguity and resemblance.

According to this interpretation, which favors and rescues the concept of leaning-on, the *object* of self-preservation is milk while that of sexuality is the breast. But milk, nourishment, is completely forgotten by the Kleinians, as well as by all who fail to see orality under two aspects. The proposition that for the human being the point from the very beginning is to incorporate the "breast," good or bad, says it all—or, rather, it says nothing.

I have borrowed a term of Lacan's, "metonymic object," which is useful here. The object, the breast, stands in a relationship of contiguity, specifically a container-contained relationship, and thus a metonymic relationship, to the mother's milk. Metonymic, certainly, but perhaps also a metaphorical relationship, destined to be caught up in the complex of metaphors and metonyms that we call symbolism. The first path of derivation, however, remains metonymic.

Furthermore, besides the distinction between milk and breast, there is detachment and divergence in this model; along the path of the arrow that turns back upon itself, it is the *breast* that is introjected in fantasy, that is "hallucinated" (I put the word in quotation marks because of my basic objections, with which you are familiar, to the notion of infantile hallucination). Hence the absurdity of speaking, apropos of the "experience of satisfaction," of the hallucinatory satisfaction of a *need*. The logic of this celebrated parable of origins puts Freud in a dilemma: either to assume that sexuality is given from the beginning, which explains nothing (this was to be the Kleinian position); or else to say that sexuality is absent at the beginning, in which case he has no adequate way to explain its advent.[62]

In the view based on emergence the *aim* is more stable. It is no longer the simple on-the-spot discharge of organ-pleasure, but a metaphorizing and transforming into fantasy of the nutritional aim. If the nutritional aim is the ingestion of food, then the sexual aim becomes the incorporation that is its derivative, this time by virtue of resemblance, or in other words metaphorically. The same goes for the aim of anality, anal expulsion being the metaphorizing of the excretion of feces.

Finally, what is the *source* in this reading that seeks to rescue leaning-on by giving it a content? It is no longer merely the "source" in the sense of an alimentary need that occasionally arouses the "sexual source." Instead it is conceived of as the alimentary—or excretory—

---

62 For a discussion of this issue, see "The Unfinished Copernican Revolution," in *Essays on Otherness*, pp. 74–78.

function as a whole, at once source, aim, and object: all the "functions serving the purpose of self-preservation" are sources that arouse zones more or less fated to become sexual.

Major problems with this endogenous/Ptolemaic interpretation

The astronomers used to speak of "saving the phenomena," by which they meant two things: to account for phenomena as best they could, or, failing that, to save face by supplying all sorts of escape routes, epicycles being one instance of this. Rescuing Freud—the goal of this commentary—means correcting the major going-astray in the conception of leaning-on—i.e., the notion of an endogenous sexuality arising from "ego" (where "ego" means the individual in question — see below, p. 77, n. 80). In Figure 3 (p. 48 above), the two arrows leave from the left—from "ego," however we conceive of it (let us say: from the organism), and by means of some sort of conjuring trick the sexual is then produced—or, more portentously, is said to "emerge"—from self-preservation, even if it is clear that someone must have put it there in the first place.

Fortunately, in the interpretation based on emergence it is the major aspects of the drive themselves (object, source, and aim) that are shaken up, or set in motion. With the parallelistic model, I was able to designate each of these aspects with a simple letter, as a reference point (Figure 3). Here, though, it is not sufficient to say that these factors are not alike, or that one arises from another. I have presented things as though one came from another, speaking of the metonymic object and the metaphorical source, but what I want to show now is not only that the *content* of the source, of the aim, and of the object derives from its counterpart in self-preservation, but also that the very concepts of source and object and aim crumble, and not just each on its own account, but each as articulated with the others.

The fact is that for each aspect, for each of these factors, we are obliged to introduce fantasy. But we must be careful, for fantasy is not simply the imagining of the real, not simply the mental side of a somatic phenomenon. Fantasy implies something other than a simple natural derivation. The path from ingestion to incorporation, and hence from the self-preservative to the sexual, is more than, and different from, a mentalization or even a symbolization.

Let us review once again the trio of source, aim, and object; this will doubtless be somewhat tiresome, but we need to get these factors into motion.

The *source* is sometimes described by reference to a specific self-preservative function, but only in a narrowly demarcated way; the locations are always a little too obvious and are in any case very few: lips, anus, external genital organs, urinary orifices—in other words, the mucous membranes, which of course should not be over-looked. The mucosae are by their nature sites of passage, subject to mechanical friction on account of what happens there, excited by the simple contact of the liquid or solid matter that passes by or through them. But they are also places of exchange with the outside, and primarily of exchange in the self-preservative sense—in other words, exchanges of the organism. They are places, too, that call for careful attention: in the animal world the places of passage and exchange constituted by the orifices of the body are also the chief sites in need of cleaning. Lastly, they are in our view the focus of something external that, taking advantage of this attention, succeeds in grafting itself onto the endogenous function.

The notion of a sexual source attached locally to a self-preservative function is even more seriously challenged when we leave behind the famous mucous membranes—the sources apropos of which it is easiest, and most canonical, to describe leaning-on. When it comes to the entire cutaneous surface as an erotogenic zone, where is the corresponding self-preservative source to be found? The same difficulty arises when Freud asserts that *any* organic function can give rise to sexual excitation.

In *Three Essays*, he even generalizes things, so far as to hypothesize that "it may well be that nothing of considerable importance can occur in the organism without contributing some component to the excitation of the sexual [drive]."[63] In "The Economic Problem of Masochism" (1924), he commented on this remark as follows: "In accordance with this, the excitation of pleasure and unpleasure would be bound to have the same result, too. The occurrence of such a libidinal sympathetic excitation [or co-excitation] when there is tension due to pain and unpleasure would be an infantile physiological mechanism which ceases to operate later on."[64]

Without involving ourselves here in Freud's discussion of masochism, it is worth noting the broadening view implied by the introduction of the idea of "co-excitation"[65] (see below, pp. 69-70). Here we are no longer concerned, as we were with leaning-on in its narrow sense, with a parallel process always arising from "ego," for it is now accepted that a disturbing factor for the organism may come from somewhere other than the self-preservative function, and that it can precipitate sexual excitation. It is clear from this what kind of generalization of the "source" is in the offing. The source becomes an exogenous agent, the implantation of a foreign body. The nature of the origin is suddenly reversed, subjected to the generalization that there is nothing endogenous that does not enshrine at least an implanted exogenous factor. The source is thus no longer a bodily site from which two processes, one self-preservative and one sexual, surge forth in tandem. If it is understood as a place from which something flows naturally, the very term "source" is no longer applicable: sexuality does not flow like water from a point of origin.

As for the *aim*, we need to understand how it too takes on a dialectical character. Even according to the famous alimentary model, the

---

63 SE VII, p. 205.
64 SE XIX, p. 163.
65 See my "Masochisme et théorie de la séduction généralisée," in *Révolution copernicienne*, esp. pp. 447–449; Eng. trans. by Luke Thurston: "Masochism and the General Theory of Seduction," in *Essays on Otherness*, esp. pp. 205–207.

shift from self-preservation to sexuality is not a simple metaphorical one: *ingestion* and *incorporation* are not mere analogs. First of all, "incorporation" means more than introducing something into the psyche: it also implies metabolizing, destroying, re-creating within oneself—all of which transcend the immediate experience of the act of eating. But there is more, too, for the *fantasy* of the oral aim goes much further. The celebrated oral triad that Bertram Lewin sought to define—eating, being eaten, and sleeping—is a far cry from a mere transformation of ingestion; notably, it implies the passive situation of being eaten, a situation that is perhaps, at the fantasy level, primordial. The sexual aim is never a mere correlative of some physiological activity.

I have been reading an ancient issue of *Nouvelle Revue de Psychanalyse* devoted to "cannibalism"—both in the anthropological sense of the term and in the sense in which psychoanalysis has, so to speak, colonized it. In this issue the only genuinely psychoanalytical article is André Green's "Cannibalisme: réalité ou fantasme agi?" (Cannibalism: Reality or Fantasy Acted Out?).[66]

In order to characterize the genesis of fantasy, Green proposes a kind of model of the experience of satisfaction, ending up, seemingly, by distinguishing two aspects: "There is good reason to draw a distinction here between the fantasy activity that occurs during the satisfaction of a drive and that which is generated in the absence, and on account of the absence, of that satisfaction."

Remember that there were also two moments in Freud's account. But the first (with the object present) was self-preservative, and no fantasy was involved. The second (absent the object) was sexual, and fantasy played a part, even if this left one wondering exactly how the sexual managed to "get into" the self-preservative.[67]

---

66 *Nouvelle Revue de Psychanalyse* 6 (Autumn 1972), pp. 27–52; quoted passages, p. 47.
67 Perhaps much in the same way as *"l'esprit vient aux filles"* (how girls grow wise)—to cite a well-known theme in bawdy literature from one of La Fontaine's tales to Colette's *Mitsou*. For a critique of the notion of the "experience of satisfaction," see "The Unfinished Copernican Revolution," in *Essays on Otherness*, pp. 74ff.

To continue quoting from Green's article (my comments in brackets): "The first type [fantasy arising along with satisfaction] would cover fantasy as the mental equivalent of the functioning of the drive (this sense is the one adopted by the Kleinians in the wake of the work of Susan Isaacs [But is this type sexual? Is there such a thing as nonsexual fantasy?]; the second type would cover fantasy properly so called [So the first type was not fantasy proper?], serving as substitute for the absent satisfaction of the drive. In this sense, in the present case we could say that it is the cannibalistic fantasy of incorporation that is incorporated instead of the breast."

How are we to understand this last sentence? Where can this fantasy of incorporation, which is destined to be—well, incorporated—actually come from? The sole meaning that can be given to what Green suggests is that it is the parental fantasy of cannibalistic incorporation that is incorporated. Unfortunately, Green did not go so far as to embrace the seduction theory. He wanted to save Isaacs and her endogenous conception and at the same time something quite different, something which, given the absence of satisfaction, should have illuminated the role of the parental message. As for the words *"au lieu du sein,"* it is worth noting that they may be read in two ways, taken to mean either "in place of the breast" or "at the site of the breast." The cannibalistic fantasy is thus said to be implanted in the body at the same place as the breast.

We thus see how the notions of source and aim are muddled by this kind of attempt to preserve leaning-on, and this goes too for the source-aim relationship. The aim is supposedly "secreted" by the source (this being the basic image of a "source," though even in the case of self-preservation it does not apply)—the aim, inasmuch as it is linked to fantasy, now suddenly assumes the role of source.

The same is true of the "object," but I will address the contradictions of the object next time. To conclude for today, let me simply quote the following passage, drawing once again from *Minutes of the Vienna Psychoanalytical Society*, specifically from Freud's reported observations from the fourth discussion of masturbation on January 24, 1912 (my comments in brackets): "Since childhood masturbation is such a general occurrence and is at the same time so poorly remembered, it must have an equivalent in psychic life. And, in fact, it is found in the fantasy encountered in most of [these] female patients [the patients in question are probably those described in the presentation at the beginning of the meeting]—namely, that the father seduced her in childhood. This is the later reworking which is designed to cover up the recollection of infantile sexual activity and represents an excuse and an extenuation thereof. The grain of truth contained in this fantasy [of seduction by the father] lies in the fact that the father, by way of his innocent caresses (*harmlosen Zärtlichkeiten*) in earliest childhood, has actually awakened the little girl's sexuality (the same thing applies to the little boy and his mother). [Notice that at this point, in 1912, Freud assigns no priority to the mother-child relationship, for he posits a perfect symmetry: father/daughter, mother/son. This will soon disappear, however.] It is these same affectionate fathers . . . who then endeavor to break the child of the habit of masturbation, of which they themselves had by that time become the unwitting cause (*die unschuldige Ursache*). And thus the motifs mingle in the most successful fashion to form this fantasy, which often dominates a woman's entire life (seduction fantasy): one part truth, one part gratification of love, and one part revenge."[68]

　　This passage is quite amusing in that it completely reverses Freud's pre-1897 theory. The father here is innocent, while the little girl is sexual. The contrast is also the opposite of Ferenczi's view: it is not the child but the adult who speaks the language of "tenderness." And Freud fails to ask himself the central question of *Three Essays*: if the father is so harmless and innocent, why does he punish masturbation? Why would he punish what he has himself provoked unless he condemns it internally? Perhaps, of course, he is innocent consciously,

---

68 Vol. IV, pp. 24–25.

but unconsciously he first represses in himself what he then proceeds to suppress in the outside world, namely sexuality.

You can see how a passage such as this, from 1912, with Freud's straying at its most egregious, continues to pay homage to the resilient truth of seduction, even if, as presented here, the seducer must be declared innocent.

February 11, 1992

Further difficulties: breaking the stranglehold of endogeny

Let me recapitulate. My purpose is to make the idea of leaning-on dialectical, and, inasmuch as it is liable to help salvage an endogenous view of the sexual drive, to break its stranglehold. With this in mind I have briefly reviewed two interpretations, one of which I call the parallelist approach, the other based on an "emergence." Last time, apropos of the latter, I tried to show for each aspect of the drive (except the object) that the concept of leaning-on cannot be salvaged without putting back into question the character not only of the sexual drive, but also of what is known as self-preservation, as well as the nature of their relationship.

We had got up to the issue of the object, and I had said that, according to the interpretation based on emergence and symbolization, the sexual object (the breast in the event) is an essentially metonymic derivative (a container with a contiguous content) of the object of the self-preservative drive, namely milk. What I now say is that this is very much the "short version." The breast is also emblematic of oral sexuality: it is not just something included in a body, but also, if I may say so without torturing the word, a *signifier*—a component of a message. I shall come back to this.

But milk, on which this account relies, is never designated by Freud as the object of feeding per se. What *is* the object of early alimentary behavior? Probably not milk alone. Does milk in its purely material nature really say much to any young animal, human or otherwise? If you put milk in a jar, not many animals will be tempted to lap it up; even a kitten needs you to stick its nose more or less in the saucer. In short, milk as such is not closely associated with a particular kind of behavior.

Let me say this, and say it even more emphatically inasmuch as I am sometimes reproached for theorizing with scant reference to actual observation: the last word here belongs entirely to ethology, not only to animal ethology but also to human—to the concrete observation of the newborn. As I stressed in *New Foundations for Psychoanalysis*, this is a frontier region for psychoanalysis, an area where it cannot find its raison d'être; human sexuality cannot be fully explained by psychoanalysis, and psychoanalysis cannot conceptualize its own object without taking into account the empirical advances of psychology, especially animal psychology. It is likely, at all events, that food is only part of an object that is a complex whole encompassing warm milk, the warm breast, and the mother; the infant seeks not just nourishment but warmth, and depends on one or more "releasers"—elaborate perceptual systems that trigger appetitive behavior. Strictly nutritional behavior can most likely be isolated only in an artificial way from other equally basic needs: the need for warmth, the need for contact, pursued by the baby by means of combinations of grasping and rooting as it strives to anchor itself in the bosom of its mother.

Between "[Drives] and Their Vicissitudes" and "On Narcissism"

In any case, when Freud claimed that the innate and predetermined nutritional object, the object of the "oral drive," is the breast, his assertion was clearly mistaken and the proposition incomplete. The breast is sucked, not ingested. At the same time, the contrary idea, as expressed in the rather abstract interpretation I reviewed last time—the idea that the object of self-preservation must be reduced to the mother's milk—is almost as badly mistaken and purely formulaic. It is false precisely because it seeks to salvage the Freudian model founded on a kind of admixture of self-preservation and sexuality—a model of the drive complete with source, aim, and object that in the end does not work for either the sexual drive or the self-preservative one. In "[Drives] and Their Vicissitudes" (1915), a rather dogmatic text, this is what Freud proposed as a definition of the drive in general, equally applicable to self-preservation and sexuality. But the model was fated to disappear shortly thereafter as part of the tendency that would lead eventually to the two great *Triebe*, the life and death drives.

In contrast to the relative dogmatism of "Vicissitudes," "On Narcissism," from 1914, is distinctly more adventurous. Admittedly, "Vicissitudes" seems to refine the issue of the *object* relative to the sexual and the self-preservative drives, but it does so on the basis of the shared model just described: "Some of the sexual [drives] are, as we know, capable of this auto-erotic satisfaction, and so are adapted to being the vehicle for the development under the dominance of the pleasure principle ... which we are about to describe [a development, therefore, without an object]. Those sexual instincts which from the outset require an object, and the needs of the ego-[drives], which are never capable of auto-erotic satisfaction, naturally disturb this state ... and so pave the way for an advance from it."[69]

What I want to underscore in this passage is not the new—and questionable—distinction between autoerotic sexual drives and sexual drives requiring an object from the outset,[70] but rather the idea that the self-preservative drives, here referred to as "ego-drives" (but I don't wish to get into this terminological issue at present), "are never capable of auto-erotic satisfaction." Of course Freud gets somewhat confused here, using the word "autoerotic" in connection with

---

69 "Instincts and Their Vicissitudes," SE XIV, p. 134, n.2.
70 In my view, *all* sexual drives are autoerotic, and all require an object from the outset.

drives that are not "erotic" at all; but one can see what he means: these are drives that are impossible to satisfy in an "auto" fashion (in or by themselves) precisely because they call for an outside object from the very start. The irrefutable idea implied here is that "self-preservative" functioning (I use quotation marks to stress that this is simply a blanket term) is *open* to the outside world from the beginning. Yet it is this non-solipsistic functioning, this openness, that is shut down in Freud's thinking when self-preservation is subsumed by the sexual model. I will come back to this later on. Even at the level of nutrition considered as a primary need—the only level that Freud and I are usually concerned with—the object is already part of a whole that implicitly includes the body of the other person, not only as a body that provides milk, but also as warmth, nesting place, and support.

What happens, though, if we try to go beyond the eternal example of the oral? If we try to trace the same sequence for anal or urinary functions, since these are supposed to offer the main examples of leaning-on subsequent to orality, can we really find anything at all, with respect to self-preservation, that resembles what Freud describes as a drive? Could feces be the *object* of a self-preservative drive—the object focused on by the excretory function? An object, moreover, that initially is barely identifiable, as we well know, since the excreta of the infant are not even a discrete *thing*—the solidified, unified fecal bolus appears only later. This consideration applies a fortiori to urination. So what exactly is this immediately present external object that Freud speaks of? And what is left of the source/aim/object scheme? And yet it is precisely in connection with anality, and solely with anality, that the word *Anlehnung* (leaning-on) appears for the very first time, in 1905, in the first edition of *Three Essays*.

What I am trying to show here might just as easily be shown apropos of urinary functioning. Not to put too fine a point on it, the idea of individualized self-preservative drives is perfectly illusory. On the one hand there are appetitive behaviors, immediately open to dialogue with the other person, the adult partner or parent; on the other hand there are needs, something very different: physiological mechanisms that in the first instance do not involve the other person, or even an "object."

If we settled for this model, what would remain of leaning-on relative to the object? Nothing, except for an impoverished derivation: food (milk) to breast. A very great deal, however, if we take the step of consulting "On Narcissism: An Introduction" (1914).

Probing "On Narcissism: An Introduction"

I propose to approach this paper from a very limited perspective only. It is a watershed text introducing immense new innovations, but these were destined, very soon, to be covered over, integrated into other wholes, or diverted. We shall to try to identify some of them later. Today, however, I shall be strictly concerned with leaning-on.

Before the publication of *The Language of Psycho-Analysis*, the only place where Freud's use of the concept of *Anlehnung* was noticed was a footnote to "On Narcissism" added by James Strachey in the *Standard Edition*. But though he thus drew attention to it, Strachey chose in his translation to use the artificial term *anaclisis/anaclitic*, which obscured everything. In this context the word appears in the expression *Anlehnungstypus der Objektwahl*: the "anaclitic" or leaning-on type of object-choice.

There is an interesting *après-coup* effect here: Freud rediscovered leaning-on in this paper of 1914, then applied the notion retrospectively to *Three Essays*, modifying the 1915 edition of that work accordingly. In fact this "leaning-on" of *Narzissmus* resembles but also differs from the original concept. Let me quote and comment on the main passage from "On Narcissism" dealing with this question: "The first auto-erotic sexual satisfactions are experienced in connection with [*im Anschluss an*] vital functions which serve the purpose of self-preservation. The sexual instincts are at the outset [leaning-on] the satisfaction of the ego-[drives]; only later do they become independent of these. . . ." Here again I would ask that you provisionally take the term "ego-drives" as synonymous with "self-preservative drives." Anyone with a (quite legitimate) curiosity about this is invited to consult the entry "Ego-Instincts" in *The Language of Psycho-Analysis*. The issue is very complicated in Freud, but for our present purposes it will suffice to conflate the two categories. Up to this point, you will have noticed, the conception of leaning-on remains just as I described it earlier. But Freud continues: "and even then we have an indication of that original attachment [leaning-on] in the fact that the persons who are concerned with a child's feeding, care, and protection become his earliest sexual objects: . . . in the first instance his mother or a substitute for her."[71]

The major role of self-preservation. The shift to "tenderness"

There has been a major shift here: all of a sudden we have left the part-object behind—along with the step-by-step interpretation of leaning-on in which I have been engaged—and been directed to the role of the other person in self-preservation; what is more, things are no longer limited to nutrition, but extend to "the persons who are concerned with a child's feeding, care, and protection." In the next few pages Freud first describes the other person, the partner in self-preservation, simply as a woman: "We say that a human being has originally two sexual objects—himself and the woman who nurses him"[72]; then, by contrast, he introduces two figures of great generality: "A person may love . . . according to the anaclitic (attachment) [leaning-on] type: (a) the woman who feeds him [and] (b) the man who protects him."[73] Feeding, care, and protection (all in all, hardly negligible requirements) are thus assigned in a rather arbitrary fash-

---

71 "On Narcissism: An Introduction," SE XIV, p. 87.
72 Ibid., p. 88.
73 Ibid., p. 90.

ion to the two aforementioned figures that I consider emblematic: why should the mother/woman not do the protecting? And obviously the man too can feed the infant—the difference between the sexes is not the issue here. Notice also who is active rather than passive: the child is not said to suck on the woman's breast; rather, it is the woman who feeds and the man who protects the child. The active role, as witness the verbs, falls to the *other person.*

All of this runs counter to the sense of the term "self-preserva-tion" and to the tendency to interpret that term in too narrow—even too "alimentary"—a fashion. At times Freud also broke self-preser-vation down into separate drives supposedly corresponding to very specific, very partial structures that are, moreover, heterogeneous and quite inadequate. The term "self-preservation," like "sexuality," is obviously part of a Freudian prosaicness that is not without its value: one must beware of sinking into pathos (though Freud would do so before long with his introduction of "Eros"). With the notion of self-preservation Freud retained a down-to-earth feeling, something indeed "alimentary," and we should not rebuke him for this out of hand: better to be prosaic than to be an intemperate *Schwärmer* or sentimentalist with overweening and grandiose pretentions. Gran-diosity was never a trait of Freud's. So much the better. But it has to be admitted that "self-preservation" falls short. On occasion Freud introduced a parallel and more eloquent antinomy, that between "affection" and "sensuality," as the two currents in love. We ran into the notion of affection or tenderness last time in the amusing passage from the *Minutes of the Vienna Psychoanalytical Society* where the topic is *Zärtlichkeiten,* the tender attentions of a father who—in all inno-cence!—seduces his child. Among psychologists the more modern term "attachment" later replaced and supplemented "tenderness." Many studies, books, and symposia were devoted to attachment, but the term has now gone out of fashion, which is perhaps a mistake.[74] In

---

74 [Note added in 2006:] This was true in 1992, but the notion is now back in fashion.

any case, all these terms encourage us not to deny something that is quite obvious, namely the vital, biological roots of animal behavior in which love itself has one of its roots.

I do not intend to discuss love today, nor for the remainder of this year. But let me just point out that for Freud love is always an admixture of three elements in variable proportions. The first of these components is tenderness as a biological factor, associated with behavior that is partly innate, partly acquired, or with phenomena such as imprinting, well described by the ethologists (recall the irreversible and touching attachment displayed by Konrad Lorenz's famous geese). The second component is of course sexuality. And the third is that subset of sexuality known as narcissism, to which we shall be returning.

Ferenczi's presentiment of the seduction theory

The notion of "tenderness" crops up in other contexts too, notably in Ferenczi, in his celebrated paper "Confusion of Tongues between Adults and the Child" (1933), in which he grasps something of what Freud repressed regarding seduction.[75]

I have often pointed out my differences with Ferenczi, and I could easily mention more, as for example something that he and Freud have in common: they are both concerned exclusively with the pathological. Like Freud, Ferenczi is limited by the assumption that the issue in question is not the constitution of the unconscious in gen-

75 In Sándor Ferenczi, *Final Contributions to the Problems and Methods of Psycho-Analysis* (London: Hogarth Press / Institute of Psycho-Analysis, 1955), pp. 156–167. A great deal of work—first of all, historical work—remains to be done on Ferenczi and seduction. To begin with, we need to know exactly what attempts he made to break open the "strongbox" of the theory of seduction that Freud rejected and left behind, especially in view of the fact that Ferenczi had access neither to the *Entwurf einer Psychologie*, the "Project for a Scientific Psychology" of 1895, nor to Freud's letters to Fliess. What exactly did he manage to dig out? There is undoubtedly a Ferenczi to be put to work in this regard—quite independently of any ambitions among Ferenczians to monopolize his work.

eral but merely pathological instances of trauma or seduction.

The "confusion of tongues" article explicitly contrasts two "languages": the language of tenderness, belonging entirely to the child, and the language of passion, belonging entirely to the adult. I find myself immediately at odds with these assignments, for there is tenderness on both sides; we need only recall, once again, the passage in the Vienna *Minutes* where tender feelings are ascribed to the father. Moreover, while there is no denying that passion (if one chooses to use this word for the sexual—although it is clearly a way of desexualizing the sexual) is predominantly on the adult side of things, what is interesting is that in Ferenczi's use the term refers to unconscious sexuality rather than sexuality openly expressed. The latter, however, is Ferenczi's chief concern: sexual abuse by the adult, overt, perverse, and traumatic—something like what Freud, in the period before 1897, referred to as seduction.

I should say, to stress my difference from Ferenczi on this point too, that in my view even with an overt act of sexual abuse, such as that performed by an adult against a child—let us say a rape—the only psychoanalytic trace that remains is an enigmatic one. An adult may subject a child to the worst outrage, yet the only place where even such a crude and overt act can be fantasized is always, and despite everything, somewhere beyond it: for the child, the question is "What does he want from me?"; for the adult, it is "What does this want from me? What came over me and made me do such a thing? What did it want from me?"

So let us come back now to the broader vision of leaning-on that opens "On Narcissism." The vital functioning referred to as self-preservation or tenderness is a complex kind of behavior with respect to which psychological and comparative observation retains all its relevance. I say "comparative" because the part of tenderness, of self-preservation, is so rapidly obscured in the human being by sexuality that it tends to be only by reference to kindred animal behavior that we manage to separate it out, this in an obviously abstract, psychological

67

sense, but a sense that is not without interest, even if it has scarcely any impact on the practice of psychoanalysts. As complex as it is, however, self-preservative functioning in even the broadest sense cannot be described as the source of the sexual, a source analogous to a natural one: we cannot say that sexuality *springs* from this overall behavior.

Self-preservation fosters tenderness; tenderness facilitates seduction

The self-preservative relationship fosters seduction, in many ways. First of all, primordially, self-preservation is open to the other person; it involves the other. Some psychoanalytical circles, especially English-speaking ones, tend to speak of interaction. Interaction is looked upon as a given and as the answer, so to speak, to everything. Whenever I ask the question "Don't you really think that the essential part of sexuality reaches the child from the other person?" I get this stonewalling answer: "Yes, of course—interaction goes both ways." All the same, despite this abuse of the notion, I am more than willing to put tenderness under the heading of interaction, just so long as all the uncertainties, lacunae, and shortcomings that have been described in the case of humans are borne in mind. It is precisely under the cover of tender interaction that the unconscious sexual aspect of the other person's message slips or insinuates itself into the child.

If we represent such child-adult interaction on the level of self-preservation as two arrows pointed at each other, the unconscious sexual aspect of the message will run parallel to the adult's behavior, as in Figure 4:

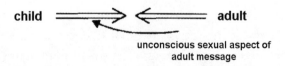

Figure 4

It is this unconscious portion of the other's message, conveyed by tender behavior itself, within the aforesaid *Zärtlichkeiten*, that is responsible somewhere in this process— wherever it affects the body and the behavior of the child—for creating the starting point for *Anlehnung* or leaning-on (assuming we want to retain the term).

The other, the adult, is various: Freud at different moments speaks of the father, the mother, the man, the woman, and of their replacements or substitutes. And above all the others, the adult in the tender relationship has multiple roles clearly distinguished by Freud: feeding, care, protection.

Third interpretation of leaning-on: priority of the adult other

In the context of a model of this kind it is perfectly illusory to try to break down the role of the adult other according to stages based on object relations. In other words, it is absurd to say that the adult may be oral, anal, or phallic in turn; this would amount merely to the reintroduction of an endogenous point of view. If, as is entirely possible, the other is anal, or phallic, or if the other is motivated and dominated by a fantasy (and he or she is inevitably dominated by fantasies), then this will remain true at any point in the other's life.

What exactly are these stages? It is impossible to conceive of them outside the relationship of tenderness and care. So let us look at them from that angle. The caregiving relationship offers and proposes points of implantation for such fantasies as the adult's actions convey. I use "implantation" in a sense that is only slightly metaphorical, because in the end I see no good reason why the fantasy and the message (i.e., the message conveying an unconscious fantasy) should not be just as easily implanted in a part of the body as in the brain.

The old idea of "co-excitation" (see p. 54 above), which does not mean quite the same thing as leaning-on, finds renewed validity here so long as it is clear that it is inseparable from fantasy: there can be no co-excitation of pain in masochism, and even perhaps no sexual co-excitation in a trauma such as a brutal bodily incident, unless an element of fantasy is involved.

Digression on "stages" or "developmentalism"

Let me return to the notion of stages, which needs to be some-what deflated. Stages are linked, as you know, to particular parts of the body: we talk about an oral stage, an anal stage, and so on, and picture the libido traveling around the body from one place to another. What then are these sites in the body? First of all, the entire body: Freud was not mistaken when he asserted that to begin with the whole body is susceptible of becoming the reception point for affectionate messages, caresses, and blandishments. But of course the parts of the body concerned are zones of transition: zones needing care, zones requiring measures of hygiene. Such zones are completely preordained, preselected by virtue of an organism's very functioning and singled out, in humans as in animals, by their need to be kept clean. What are we to think, then, of the notions of successive stages keyed to a succession of locations and of a libido following a zigzag route through the body to each zone in turn?

There is something ridiculous about what have been called "stages" in psychoanalysis. As a matter of fact, Freud never really espoused the idea of a succession of such stages, some even subdi-vided; the scheme was actually the brainchild of Karl Abraham. I refer you to an excellent article on Abraham by Rosolato and Widlöcher[76]; though already old, for it dates from 1958, it offers a clear account of Abraham's unapologetic "stageism," in which everything is subdi-vided on a scalar model, not only the libidinal stages, but also those of the ego and those in the progression of object-choice. Abraham splits the oral stage into sucking and biting substages and the anal stage

---

76 Guy Rosolato and Daniel Widlöcher, "Karl Abraham: lecture de son oeuvre," *La Psychanalyse* 4 (Paris: PUF, 1958), pp.153–178.

into phases dominated by expulsion and retention respectively, and so on. Certainly we must be honest enough to acknowledge that certain physiological maturational steps are important, but their main importance from our point of view lies precisely in the fact that they focus the attention of the adult and inflect his or her gestures, messages, and fantasies. This applies to teething, for example, and even more to the maturational step of "sphincter control," leading to better retained and more solid stool. This is all obvious, but it by no means justifies ranking self-preservative stages in a set order, much less postulating the existence of corresponding libidinal stages, or stages of the ego, or stages of object-choice, not to say stages in the scientific comprehension of the world!

Ferenczi himself fell into this trap in his "Stages in the Development of the Sense of Reality" (1913).[77] Where does schematizing everything in this way lead us? The answer is simple: to a psychoanalysis based on multiple-choice questions. "What comes after oral stage 2? Is it (1) the anal stage? or (2) the urethral stage?" A sort of psychoanalysis for raw recruits! Which puts me in mind of a stupid joke: "What are the feet?" an adjutant asks the soldiers he is training. Each is supposed to answer, and each naturally gets it wrong: the feet are a means of locomotion, the feet are the lowest extremity of the body, and so on. The officer, consulting his manual, gives the correct answer: no, the feet are not a means of locomotion, they are "the object of the soldier's continual vigilance." The adjutant's answer, for all its absurdity, is far more interesting than the answers of his recruits. For us, here, it is a reminder that *all* these bodily zones call for an adult's care, for the attentions that are given from the first hours of life and to which it is perfectly vain to posit an order of priority. From the first hours of life the anal and genital zones are the object of the vigilance not of the soldier but of the person who cares for the child, usually the

---

77 Eng. trans. by Ernest Jones, in *Contributions to Psycho-Analysis* (Boston: Badger, 1916 [later editions titled *Sex and Psychoanalysis* and *First Contributions to Psycho-Analysis*]).

mother. This is not to deny that sequences, successive polarizations, are established. But even in the matter of what we call toilet training, to which I referred a moment ago apropos of the development of sphincter control (meaning at first a more relaxed anal behavior and then a more controlled one), everyone knows how this learning process varies from one child to the next, and that it certainly does not come about solely in accordance with the child's muscular or even neurological maturation, but also in accordance with what the parents supply by way of vigilant attention. As with the soldier, so with the mother. That is what creates the erotogenic zones.

Enter the adult other

The erotogenic zones, then, are the object of attentions permeated by the adult caretaker's major fantasies. The nursing mother is able right away to "stuff" a phallic or anal breast into her child, and she has no need to wait for the phallic or anal stage. Let me remind you of the marvelous slip that we found in Freud's "Project for a Scientific Psychology" (1895): instead of writing *Nahrungszufuhr*, the provision of food, Freud wrote *Nahrungseinfuhr*, the introduction of food.[78] Quite apt for us, since we are commenting on *Zur Einführung des Narzissmus* (literally, "on the introduction of narcissism"). The beauty of this slip of Freud's is that it perfectly describes the action of the adult, which goes far beyond the presentation or offering of food to the child, which any neutral and anonymous service might do.

The care lavished on the child concentrates on erotogenic zones and delimits them; it likewise concentrates on and delimits signifiers on the body of the adult—the breast, for instance. Among the ideas to be elaborated in a long-awaited book by Jacqueline Lanouzière is one that psychoanalysts have all neglected: they have apparently for-

---

78 See "The Unfinished Copernican Revolution," in *Essays on Otherness*, p. 75, n. 49, and p. 77, n. 63.

gotten that the breast is an erotogenic zone in adults! You can read everything by Melanie Klein without ever coming across the idea that the breast is an object of pleasure, that women actually derive pleasure from it. The breast is the prize exhibit of the Kleinians (and of a few others), yet it is never described as a site of pleasure (I say never, but perhaps I ought not to, and should anyone find an instance, I would be only too happy!).

As for the idea of leaning-on, I tried to subvert it, to reorient it by means of seduction. But instead seduction overturned the whole structure of leaning-on: I persisted nevertheless, for the self-preservative or tender relationship could not be defined in terms of drives on the old model. This holds a fortiori for the sexual drive—assuming we wish to retain the term "drive" in this case.[79] Since we do so wish, we certainly cannot do it without completely upsetting Freud's famous four aspects of the drive. In particular, the sexual drive has a *source* that is at once—and inextricably—a fantasy and something implanted in the body by the adult other. Thus the drive's object, the other person, is at the drive's origin. Its source-object (and we might even say its source-object-aim) is the remnant of the enigmatic content that parasitizes the adult's communications, communications that otherwise serve self-preservation.

Enigmatic: let me end for today with this word. I am delighted to say that it is meeting with success. The next posthumous work of Léon Chertok, a collection of articles, is to be entitled *L'énigme au coeur de la médecine* (The Enigma at the Heart of Medicine). I am happy to see that the enigma is making its way.

---

79 *La pulsion pour quoi faire?* (The Drive for What Reason?) is the title of a collective work by Didier Anzieu, Roger Dorey, Jean Laplanche, and Daniel Widlöcher (Paris: Association Psychanalytique de France, 1984).

February 18, 1992

We are following the complicated, zigzag trajectory of a straying from the path, and this is all the more complicated in that we are tracing the thought of a genius who from time to time corrects course in the most extraordinary fashion. There are continual additions (we will examine some shortly) and revisions based on psychoanalytic experience (*die psychoanalytische Erfahrung*), and there are sudden, almost kaleidoscopic shifts that have raised many issues, by no means all of them unproductive. To correct straying while retaining its contributions and innovations is no less complicated. Is it possible to show what psychoanalytic theory could be, or could have been, without the initial straying? Does not deconstructing all these aporias amount to laying new and different foundations for psychoanalysis?

Seduction explodes the notion of leaning-on

I have endeavored to show the new meaning that leaning-on could have once placed in the framework of the seduction theory, which certainly means removing it from its original context—that of an endogenous process in which the sexual drive emerges from self-preservation—but which also means taking into account new elements in the development of Freud's thought. In other words, not only does the notion of leaning-on explode on account of its internal contradictions (as I have tried to argue by demonstrating that its only possible interpretation—its truth, so to speak—involves the idea of seduction), but also—and this time the argument comes from Freud—a new element broadens this perspective with the introduction of the "leaning-on" type of object-choice (*Anlehnungstypus der Objektwahl*). This has enabled us to form a new picture of things, especially with respect to the object.

A somewhat simplistic theory held that the object in question was the object of the self-preservative functions. We concluded to the contrary that the leaning-on type of object-choice reveals and is directed at something far transcending food, specifically milk, as a purely material object: the actual context of the object of self-preservation is the entirety of what is rightly called attachment, and which Freud sometimes called tenderness. Further, we came to see that the sexual object, in its essence a fantasy object (for at the beginning that object, for instance the breast, can be an object only in fantasy), is not just an associative derivative of milk. That is too simple, even if it is true on one level to say that the sexual object stands in a metonymic relationship to the nutritional one. As I have tried to show, we must go further, and grasp who it is that *designates* this transition from milk to breast, who it is that de-signs, delimits, and circumscribes something which is the breast, the mother's breast, identified *by that mother herself* as a sexual organ of her own and as the core of her attachment relationship with the child, a relationship which (as I have emphasized) is well and truly interactive in its own terms.

Return to "narcissism": the ego and the drives

Now let me continue to trace Freud's straying with regard to drives, the continual allure for him of an endogenous biologism, even a meta-biologism, that tempted him ever more insistently as he proceeded. Let me return to "On Narcissism: An Introduction," from 1914, confining myself so far as I can to its concern with drives. This is a decidedly difficult text, a research text, as much by virtue of the ideas it introduces as of those it synthesizes; aside from narcissism, it introduces among other notions the ideal, the superego, and a theory of hypochondria. The paper is rife with discoveries and clarifications. Today I will approach it from the standpoint of what is after all its main theme, namely the introduction of narcissism.

Introducing narcissism obviously means reintroducing the ego, and reintroducing it into psychoanalytic theory. And we know all that was to become of the notion of the ego thereafter, with *The Ego and the Id* (1923) and the whole history of what has been called ego psychology, to mention just that. (I refer you to the entry "Ego" in *The Language of Psycho-Analysis*, a text which, once again, I can see no way to improve on; it is the longest entry in that work, and it offers a good account of the development of the notion of the ego with its problems—its problematic—from the outset and throughout Freud's work. Here I shall merely stress a few points, adding just a little, per-haps, to the discussion in *The Language of Psycho-Analysis*, which is already quite thorough.)

First of all there is the useful distinction—helpful in getting one's bearings, even though it must quickly be abandoned—between the ego qua individual and the ego qua agency[80]: between the indi-vidual we might describe as biopsychic, in the sense that we might call an animal a biopsychic individual, and what we call the *moi-instance*, the agency of the ego. Henceforward Freud would use the word *Instanz* in this connection; it has the legal connotation, as we noted in *The Language of Psycho-Analysis* (s.v. "Agency"), of a judging or censoring authority, and first appeared in Freud's writings as early as *The Interpretation of Dreams* (1900). The English "agency," while it does not quite have the judicial resonance of the German *Instanz* or the French *instance*, clearly implies a delegation of powers, a "repre-

---

80 To be distinguished from what I sometimes call *ego*, a term I introduced for the sake of convenience [as opposed, that is, to the French translation of *das Ich*, which is *le moi*. –Trans.]. I use *ego*, in particular contexts, to denote *the one in question*—a locus, in other words, that implies nothing as to whether it is filled by an individual, a per-son, a subject, etc. So, for example, instead of saying Henry or Paul, I simply say *ego*.

sentative" function. What Pontalis and I clearly demonstrated was that the two meanings of the ego, as individual and as agency, were present in Freud from the beginning, *pace* the simplistic but persistent claim that Freud spoke of the ego as an individual until about 1914 and then, all of a sudden, proceeded to give it a completely different—topographical—meaning. In reality, both the distinction and the relationship between the two had always been there. For, obviously, if the two were quite distinct, it would have sufficed to use two different terms—to call the first "the individual," for instance, and that would have been that. But that was not that, for the precise reason that there is interplay between the ego as individual and the ego as the individual's delegated agency.

Metonymic and metaphorical derivations of the ego

But what is the nature of that relationship of delegation between individual and agency? I have stressed the fact that there are only two forms of delegation, as there are of association in general: contiguity and resemblance, or in other words metonymy and metaphor. In "The Derivation of Psychoanalytic Entities"[81] I took as an example the question of the derivation of the ego-as-agency, at once metonymic and metaphorical, from the ego-as-individual. I pointed out that a double derivation like this extends well beyond the realms of logic, of rhetoric, or of the mental, for one could say in the same way that on the biological level the child is a metonymic derivative, a piece of the mother's body, and that at the same time, as the image of his mother or parents, he is also a metaphorical derivative. Thus generation itself cannot avoid these two great and unique pathways of derivation. But this too offers the possibility of a kind of oversimplification, which I have in the past sought to rectify, in the sense that

---

81 "Dérivation des entités psychanalytiques" [1971], in *Révolution copernicienne*, pp. 107–124. Eng. trans. by Jeffrey Mehlman: Appendix to *Life and Death*, pp. 127–139.

it is not a matter of drawing a distinction once again between two "egos," one metonymic, the other metaphorical. The problem is that one and the same ego is both metonymic and metaphorical, metonymo-metaphorical as it were, and derives in a complex manner from something that could be described as the totality of a living organism in the world. So we must speak not of a metonymic ego or of a metaphorical ego, but rather of the ego's metonymic derivation and its metaphorical derivation.

What is meant by the metonymic derivation of the ego? The term "agency" suggests the answer: a kind of differentiated organ, a specialization within the whole, responsible for one of that whole's functions. As with a minister in a government, a government in a country, or some particular constituted body, what is involved is a differentiated component, a part of the organism to which a particular function is delegated. And we know Freud leaned very far in this direction, toward metonymy and specialization, because he tells us that the ego and the perception-consciousness system from which it stems (or which, if you prefer, is its center) are a differentiated part of the organism, though a differentiation on the organism's surface only—ultimately a sort of skin, or eye, an organ of reception and protection. This account of the development of the ego and of the perception-consciousness system may be found, for example, in *Beyond the Pleasure Principle* (1920).[82] But then we also have a little, seemingly mysterious observation in *The Ego and the Id* (1923), which has been pointed out by many people, including me, and which indeed has been made into a cardinal point of the thinking of Didier Anzieu: the ego, Freud writes, "is not merely a surface entity, but is itself the projection of a surface."[83] Which means precisely that the ego is not only metonymic in character, but also metaphorical. Not just a differentiated, surface portion of the mental apparatus but also something

---

82 SE XVIII, pp. 1–64.
83 SE XIX, p. 26 and note 1.

like the projection of the surface, so to speak, something that, from within, resembles the surface. The term "projection" is taken here in all its meanings, including the original meaning given it by Freud the neurologist, the well-known sense in which we picture a "homunculus"—the "projection" of the various parts of the body—inscribed on the cerebral cortex. Freud is clearly referring to this—complete with a set of "correlations" that might well be described as fantastical. For instance, there is a sort of back-and-forth or interplay in Freud's thinking between the two kinds of surface covered by what he called a "surface entity," conceived of at once as a sort of bark, and on the other as the cerebral cortex, which (etymology notwithstanding) has nothing bark-like about it, being on the contrary hypersensitive and quite delicate.

The ego and the self

All the same, to take the long view of the fate of concept of the ego both in Freud's work and in that of his successors (especially those who defined it in the terms of "ego psychology"), it was the metonymic aspect that prevailed: the ego came to be viewed as a differentiation, an apparatus or organ responsible for reason, rationality, and mastery of the drives, as well as a means of negotiating between the drives and the outside world. The ego's metaphorical derivation was thus pushed aside, making it at best difficult for authors to keep the two derivations in mind simultaneously: on the one hand the notion of the ego as an organ of rationality, perception, and consciousness, and on the other hand that of an ego with the form of something possibly more obscure and less rational. It is fair to say that this accounts for the introduction of the idea of the "self." The justification (or rather the pretext) for this was indeed an inability to let the two derivations coexist. Inasmuch as the ego was reduced to a purely rational agency, Cartesian if not ultimately Platonic (recall Plato's νοῦς restraining the passions), room needed to be found for another factor, and here identifications were the answer. It is hard, though, to accept that identifications, very possibly distorted, can provide the foundation for an agency charged with telling true from false. These considerations alone explain the invention as well as the present hypertrophy of the identificatory and metaphorical agency of the *self*, which, as I have often noted, was brought in to free the ego from the irrationality of which it is also the bearer.

Here, then, are two distinctions, both too facile, that might be said to duplicate each other: the distinction between an ego and a self, or—as I have been urged to say but will not—between a metonymic ego and a metaphorical ego (which is exactly the same antithesis), replicating and exacerbating the equally classificatory and extrinsic contrast between ego-as-individual and ego-as-agency.

The principal explicit forerunners of "On Narcissism" (1914) are Freud's book on Leonardo da Vinci (1910), with its underlying debate with Isidor Sadger over the problem of narcissistic identification with the mother,[84] and his study of the case of Schreber (1911), where this time the figure looming in the background is Carl Jung.[85]

So-called "primary" narcissism as a secondary state . . .

It is interesting to read a first "introduction to narcissism" in the Schreber study, written three years before "On Narcissism" (comments in brackets are mine):

> Recent investigations [Freud is referring to Sadger and to his own *Leonardo*] have directed our attention to a stage [we shall be returning to the term *stage* to discuss and challenge it] in the development of the libido which it passes through on the

---

84 *Leonardo da Vinci and a Memory of His Childhood*, SE XI, pp. 57–137.
85 "Psycho-Analytic Notes on an Autobiographical Account of a Case of Paranoia (Dementia Paranoides)" (hereafter "Schreber Case"), SE XII, pp. 1–82.

way from auto-erotism to object-love. [That libido shifted from autoerotism to object-love had been maintained by Freud since 1905: autoerotism in childhood, object-love in puberty and adulthood.] This stage has been described as *"Narzissismus"*; I prefer to give it the name of *"Narzissmus"*, which may not be so correct, but is shorter and less cacophonous.[86] What happens is this. There comes a time in the development of the individual [this account is interesting, being more explicit on this point than Freud's text of 1914] at which he unifies his sexual [drives] (which have hitherto been engaged in auto-erotic activities) in order to obtain a love-object; and he begins by taking himself [*sich selbst nimmt*], his own body, as his love-object [here we may note the appearance of something akin to the *Selbst*, a predecessor of the "self"—but this is a "body-self"], and only subsequently proceeds from this to the choice of some person other than himself as his object. This half-way phase between auto-erotism and object-love may perhaps be indispensable normally [in Freud, despite everything, we often encounter the idea of a goal-directed and

---

86 Note that Freud's preference was not echoed in the French (*narcissisme*) [or English (*narcissism*)] translations of the term, also chosen as more assonant. As a matter of fact, some people have proposed a psychoanalytic interpretation of Freud's choice, arguing that his elimination of the syllable *"is"* from the word *Narzissismus*, just like his elimination of the same syllable from his forename Sigismund, reflected a repression on his part of the name of the goddess Isis, or in other words a whole aspect of Egyptology. Whatever one may think of this psychoanalytic hypothesis about Freud, on which I have no wish to comment, there is no getting away from the fact that clipping a syllable from one's own first name is not nothing! On this issue, see Ricardo Andrade's thesis, defended at the University of Paris VII on December 12, 1990: *L'héritage romantique allemand dans la pensée freudienne* (The Heritage of German Romanticism in Freudian Thought).

normative succession]; but it appears that many people linger unusually long in this condition, and that many of its features are carried over by them into the later stages of their development. [A point, then, where development comes to a halt, a place of fixation, and hence a locus of possible regression.] What is of chief importance in the subject's self [here what we have is *das Selbst: an diesem Selbst*] thus chosen as a love-object may already be the genitals. The line of development then leads on to the choice of an external object with similar genitals—that is, to homosexual object-choice—and thence to heterosexuality. [A sort of normal sequence is thus suggested: autoerotism, narcissism, homosexual object-choice, heterosexual object-choice, with potential stopping places all along the way.][87]

The two clinical studies in which Freud approaches the question of narcissism—and you will immediately notice that they are clinical approaches to texts, not to actual courses of treatment—are, first, his study of Leonardo and, second, his analysis of Senatspräsident Dr. Schreber. Let me simply remind you of some well-known details. Freud defines Leonardo's homosexuality as a narcissistic object-choice: having been too much loved by his mother, Leonardo puts himself in her place so as to love young men as he himself was loved by her when he was young. He thus chooses objects on the model of what he once was, but in doing so he places himself, as lover, in a different position, namely that of the mother.

Freud's other broaching of the issue of narcissism came apropos of the case of Dr. Schreber, the subject of continual and marveling discussion with Jung in the correspondence between the two men.

---

87 "Schreber Case," SE XII, pp. 60–61.

Freud's interpretation here was that after the disaster or "catastrophe" of his loss of the world and of objects, Schreber reconstructed himself by means of delusions of grandeur, building a closed but grandiose universe. Here is what Freud had to say in "On Narcissism" (my comments again in brackets): "What happens to the libido which has been withdrawn from external objects in schizophrenia? The megalomania characteristic of these states points the way. This megalomania has no doubt come into being at the expense of object-libido. The libido that has been withdrawn from the external world has been directed to the ego and thus gives rise to an attitude which may be called narcissism. But the megalomania itself is no new creation; on the contrary, it is, as we know, a magnification and plainer manifestation of a condition which had already existed previously. [This passage is notable in that it states clearly that psychosis is a secondary narcissism, a regression to a primary narcissism, and that the primary narcissism thus returned to is that of childhood. Secondary narcissism is an adult phenomenon, pathological or symptomatic; primary narcissism is, quite simply, the narcissism of childhood. This helps demystify the notion of a primary narcissism said to characterize the 'origins.' Freud continues:] This leads us to look upon the narcissism which arises through the drawing in of object-[investments] as a secondary one, superimposed upon a primary narcissism that is obscured by a number of different influences."[88]

. . . an idea that Freud would later muddy

It should be emphasized that this distinction between secondary and primary underwent a shift later, when Freud applied the term "primary narcissism" to a kind of narcissism of the biological individual, or in other words to a primal biological state, a state that ultimately was not mental, while using "secondary narcissism" for a "narcissism of the ego"—a love directed even in childhood at the agency of the

---

88 "On Narcissism," SE XIV, pp. 74–75.

ego. The shift is retrogressive, embracing a state that might be said to be invented, an original biological state that is an absolutely unwarranted postulate. (I have often crossed swords with defenders of this notion of a primal biological narcissism.) This shift in meaning, as you will have noticed, is not reflected in the text I have just quoted, where secondary narcissism is quite clearly the narcissism of narcissistic symptoms, while primary narcissism is the narcissism of childhood—the narcissism that *follows* autoerotism and so is not truly primary, as it does not exist at the very outset of the human being's development.

The introduction of this concept of narcissism was a moment so powerful, so new, that it caused tremors in the theory of the drives as a whole. Tremors that implied far more than formal issues and called for a truly radical response: "In the total absence of any theory of the [drives] which would help us to find our bearings, we may be permitted, or rather, it is incumbent upon us, to start off by working out some hypothesis to its logical conclusion, until it either breaks down or is confirmed."[89]

Naturally, we can choose in this text between what foreshadows the straying to come and what carries the seeds of something more fruitful. For the moment I prefer to focus on what seems to me more fruitful. With this in mind allow me to quote a key passage from "On Narcissism," one that in the end merely reiterates the long extract from the Schreber case that I quoted earlier: "I may point out that we are bound to suppose that a unity comparable to the ego cannot exist in the individual from the start; the ego has to be developed. The auto-erotic [drives], however, are there from the very first; so there must be something added to auto-erotism—a new psychical action—in order to bring about narcissism."[90]

This passage has often been discussed; I myself have stressed that saying "the auto-erotic drives are there from the very first" is

89 Ibid., p. 78.
90 Ibid., pp. 76–77.

already a kind of flattening out, for elsewhere, notably in *Three Essays,* Freud explicitly states that "the drive becomes auto-erotic." In fact, therefore, this narcissism succeeds autoerotism, which must *itself* succeed an earlier moment because autoerotism, as a recourse to fantasy, is something that *arises at some point.*

This first narcissism, "primary" as it may be, nevertheless comes second. Not in the sense that it comes after some other narcissism, but in the sense that it comes after something else. There is a terminological ambiguity here that needs to be dispelled: do we say primary by reference to something secondary, to a later narcissism, or do we mean primary in an absolute sense, in the sense that nothing precedes it? For me it is clear that we are concerned with a primary narcissism, but one that is not the first moment of "development" (to talk like Freud—but there is no good reason to reject this temporal way of thinking).

Narcissistic stage or narcissistic moments?

Let me return for a moment to the term "stage." Nothing obliges us to view this first narcissism as a stage. I would even argue that the sequence proposed by Freud—autoerotism, narcissism, homosexual object-choice, heterosexual object-choice—is a kind of abstract lineage that has never given rise to anything much in later psychoanalytic thought. One would be hard pressed to harmonize this "canonical" developmental sequence with other sequences, for example the succession of libidinal stages. The failure of the stage-ist approach is even more apparent in this case. For my own part, seeing no need to treat narcissism as a stage, I am tempted rather to see it manifesting itself in a host of narcissistic *moments*—without, however, denying the existence of repeated micro-sequences, as when autoerotism is followed by narcissism. Generally speaking, for the human being there is no more a narcissistic "stage" than there is an autoerotic one.

Ego-unifying factors: Federn, Lacan, Anzieu

As for Freud's expression "a new psychical action," I feel we ought to speak rather of "new psychical *actions*" to be "added to auto-erotism." In this connection a host of authors with many different approaches have sought to complete a picture only sketched by Freud. Let me mention three names: Ernst Federn, who addressed the problem of the ego's unifying function, and, on the ego's genesis, Jacques Lacan and Didier Anzieu.

With regard to Lacan, the issue, naturally, is the notion of the "mirror stage,"[91] a notion whose actual creator, as we are repeatedly reminded, was Henri Wallon. I confess that this type of criticism leaves me cold, because what Lacan did with this idea is not what Wallon did with it. Perhaps Lacan was remiss in failing to give his sources, but the source, after all, is not the whole river.

Even Lacan does not entirely avoid stageism, and this not simply in the title of his article, but also in its content: the idea that everything happens one day, in a given month, at a certain moment, all of a sudden. His description of the mirror stage has a highly dramatic character: one fine day, as it were, the mayonnaise takes.

As for the "mirror," while Lacan does not say so explicitly, his mirror stage can easily dispense with the actual device we call a mirror. People who have never had a mirror at their disposal, or even a reflecting surface, are perfectly apt to go through the mirror stage. The mirror in question is the mirror image of *the other*.[92] Lacan further offers the idea of something "jelling": even if not necessarily

---

91 Jacques Lacan, "Le stade du miroir comme formateur de la fonction du Je" (1949), in *Écrits* (Paris: Seuil, 1966), pp. 93–100; Eng. trans. by Bruce Fink: "The Mirror Stage as Formative of the I Function," in Écrits *Complete in English*, pp. 75–81.

92 This idea is present also in Freud: in his discussion of the case of Schreber he uses the term *Spiegelung*, or mirror image, sometimes translated as "reflection"—incorrectly, for a reflection implies something evanescent. In the passage from the Schreber case to which I refer, Freud observes that in myths the sun's "counterpart [*Spiegelung*] in [the] picture of the two parents is 'Mother Earth.'" (SE XII, p. 54).

at the first attempt, there is something that at a given moment turns or shifts. This was a period when Lacan could devote an entire lecture to the phenomenon of imprinting in animals (an idea that I myself met with for the first time in that context): he would cite ovulation in the female pigeon when confronted by the *Gestalt* of the male, or the transformation of desert locusts from the solitary to the gregarious form, as triggered here too by a specular phenomenon. Obviously, neither desert locusts nor pigeons need a mirror to go through a "mirror stage." Of course, it is also possible to precipitate ovulation in a female pigeon by showing her an image of herself in a mirror. But what Lacan is talking about is the image of the counterpart, not necessarily such an image recognized on a reflecting surface.

With Didier Anzieu we are presented with a train of thought seemingly rather different, but which to my mind is complementary. The key term here is "skin-ego."[93] The idea of the skin-ego is indeed that the ego is not only a surface but also the projection of a surface; it is metaphorically the skin of the psyche or, as Anzieu also says, "a skin for thoughts." The ego coheres thanks to the projection of the body's surface.

These two approaches, Lacan's and Anzieu's, are in fact by no means contradictory. It is easy, for example, to conceive of the mirror of the mirror stage as also a tactile mirror, for one's skin perceives itself only by touching the skin of another person, or else by touching some part of one's own body *as if* it were another person's body. The idea that the ego derives from an essentially visual imprinting, or from other sensory pathways, notably tactile ones, can only enhance our understanding of the genesis of the ego as agency.

---

93 See Didier Anzieu, *Le moi-peau* (Paris: Dunod, 1985); Eng. trans. by Chris Turner: *The Skin Ego* (New Haven and London: Yale University Press, 1989).

Narcissism and narcissistic object-choice

What I myself have been able to contribute to this discussion is in the first place the idea that there is no temporal priority as between narcissism (the narcissistic phase or moment) on the one hand and "narcissistic object-choice" on the other. What one might suspect from reading Freud's "Mourning and Melancholia" (1915)[94] and his *Leonardo* is that the original narcissism is *nothing but* narcissistic object-choice: the two crystallize together, for specular reciprocity must be firmly maintained at any moment of totalization.[95]

Narcissism so understood is love for the ego, for an ego itself precipitated by love, just at the moment when love is felt for the *Gestalt* of the counterpart, just as the living being attaches itself to that mirror image. Freud tells us that this ego is loved, is invested by libido, and indeed turns into "a great reservoir of libido." Meanwhile the ego is also a "binding" force: it binds, it is by definition total, its task

---

94 SE XIX, pp. 237–258.

95 I would add the following. It is by no means inevitable that an individual should recognize himself in a mirror. Look at your own image in a looking-glass along with a photograph of yourself. Compare the two, and you will notice a certain incongruity, because the mirror reverses what you see in the photograph. This does not amount to much, of course: you recognize your own image in both cases, but there is a discrepancy. Why? The fact is that there are certain asymmetrical features in any face. Suppose for the sake of argument that human beings were not symmetrical at all—which is conceivable, since asymmetrical beings do exist, even though symmetry is by far the more usual case. In that event they would not be able to recognize themselves in the mirror: an asymmetrical living being could not perceive the other here as like himself, and "another himself" could not, a priori, be identical to his mirror image. If I am going a bit too fast here, I refer you, for example, regarding the basic identity of primary narcissism and narcissistic object-choice, to my discussion in *Problématiques I*, especially apropos of the passage about "His Majesty the Baby" in "On Narcissism" (SE XIX, p. 91), where one senses Freud's text suddenly reversing gear by implying that behind the baby-for-the-adult lies the adult-for-the-baby. See *Problématiques I: L'angoisse* (Paris: PUF, 1980), pp. 305–306 and 32–21; also, regarding Leonardo's painting of St. Anne (SE XI, pp. 111ff.), *Problématiques III: La sublimation* (Paris: PUF, 1980), pp. 87–88—a subject, moreover, that has been thoroughly dealt with by J.-P. Maïdani-Gérard in *Léonardo da Vinci: mythologie ou théologie?* (Paris: PUF, 1994).

is to keep things together, to assemble all its autoerotic drives and at the same time to contain them, to contain autoerotism: to contain the erotic, and ultimately to enshroud and totalize it, but at the same time to moderate it and exercise mastery over it in a marginal or lateral way. This idea dates back to the "Project for a Scientific Psychology" (1895), where it is expounded in terms of "neurones," but remains suggestive with regard to the mechanics of the psyche.[96] The ego, says Freud in the Project, is like a network of invested neurones; this group of neurones is more highly charged than are those external to it, so that any process in close proximity to the ego finds itself attracted to and enveloped by the totality, moderated or slowed down instead of flowing freely, as if by a sort of magnetism. By analogy with the findings of modern astronomy, one might say that everything that occurs near the "black hole" of the ego is suddenly pulled into its mass. This is an image by no means outdated from the standpoint of the psychology of the neuroses and of the symptom.

What we have, then, is an ego that is loved: the ego that binds and sustains the erotic; but also an ego that loves, for it will eventually find an object for itself that is modeled on itself. And it is at this point that the second type of object-choice comes into play, following on the "leaning-on type of object-choice" (*Anlehnungstypus* of *Objektwahl*) and described by Freud as "the narcissistic type of object-choice." The love-object is now chosen on the model of the ego itself, in accordance with the celebrated options listed by Freud: what one is (oneself); (2) what one once was (oneself); (3) what one would like to be (oneself); (4) a part of one's own self.[97] All cases involve the *Selbst*. One might say that the ego is seen here in its "reflexive" form, as oneself or as the "self."

The entries on these two types of object-choice in *The Language of Psycho-Analysis* showed the apparent contradictions in Freud's text.[98]

---

96 SE I, pp. 281–397, especially pp. 322ff.
97 "On Narcissism," SE XIV, p. 90.
98 *S.v.* "Anaclitic Type of Object-Choice" and "Narcissistic Object-Choice."

But in point of fact these issues go *beyond* contradictions, for neither of the two types of choice can really be described without reference to the other, and the two are in fact truly inextricable. The main illustration of this is that, in love, the man's choice of a woman is par excellence an object-choice based upon leaning-on (a non-narcissistic choice); yet by making it he unburdens himself, precisely, of his own narcissism; furthermore, he is attracted by someone who is herself narcissistic. You see how intimately linked the two types are—how complicated their description is but how close in fact to experience.

Towards a theory of love?

Obviously, what is heaving into view here is a theory of love in which the narcissistic factor plays a large part. Psychoanalysis is justified in attempting to unmask narcissism in the passion of love, and Freud himself suggested this approach, as for instance in "[Drives] and Their Vicissitudes" (1915), where he introduces the distinction between love and hate by pointing out that we cannot attribute love or hate to the drives, that it is quite absurd to say that a drive "loves" or "hates" its object; a drive neither loves nor hates, and we therefore speak of love and hate only with reference to total persons as they relate to total objects.[99] Nor are we far away here from the old Eros of Aristophanes, which I have already mentioned and will have occasion to mention again.

Let me finish for today by stressing that this long passage from "On Narcissism" concerning the two types of object-choice and their interrelatedness is one of the main texts in Freud's work that deals with love, a text that is revisited too infrequently, even in Freud's work itself. I have had occasion to note that an article such as "Observations on Transference-Love" (1914) makes no allusion to this

---

99 "Instincts and Their Vicissitudes," SE XIV, p. 137.

distinction despite the light it might have shed on the matter.[100] If we are to reconsider the question of love, then it must undoubtedly be tackled from not two but three angles: first, tenderness or the relationship of self-preservative attachment; second, erotic elements properly so-called; and, last, the level of narcissistic Eros.

It is with these three levels that I will start next time, in an attempt to show the way that leads from the ultimately very unstable balance described in "On Narcissism" to a new disequilibrium and a certain backtracking, which some have gone so far as to deem delusional, and which falls under the heading of the life and death drives.

---

100 SE XII, pp. 156–171.

February 25, 1992

So what I am trying to do is reconstruct a sort of ideal moment based on an "ideal" view of "On Narcissism" as it might have been had the initial going-astray of 1897 never occurred.

General view: three models

Figure 5 shows three models that vary greatly with respect to the object and the partner or other.

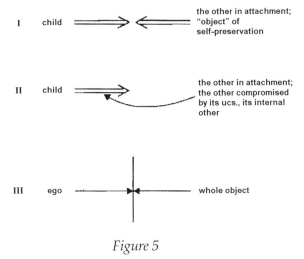

Figure 5

I describe Model I as that of attachment and self-preservation. The two are closely linked, the term "self-preservation" on its own being inadequate to account for the complexity of each phase of the process, especially with respect to the object, because to define the object as purely and simply nutritional is to ignore an entire structure, a feature of animal life in the noblest sense, namely the attachment of the young to the parent—usually, but by no means always, to the mother.

Model II represents sexuality, which may be described as "erotic" without tautology for the simple reason that it was in terms of the erotic that Freud first illuminated sexuality in his *Three Essays* (1905). You can see that the articulation of II with I depends on seduction and on the leaning-on that results from it, as discussed earlier. The arrow of attachment *designates* the other person, but that other is not actually as simple as attachment would like to think (so to speak); instead, the other person is "compromised" by their own unconscious—by their own "internal" other, one might say—so that the messages the other sends are themselves compromised, or "enigmatic," to use that term once more. Let me define this "erotic sexuality" a little: it is a sexuality that constitutes itself in fantasy and in fantasy only, that originates in the unconscious, and that is not bound—which is to say not unified—with respect either to its zones and objects or to its manifestations and aims. It is what Freud calls "autoerotic"—a term that is unclear to Freud himself, and I say this because "autoerotic" does not connote everything that the notion of sexuality is meant to connote.

Lastly, Model III encapsulates Freud's additions of 1911–1914: the advent or discovery of narcissistic sexuality, bound and binding, and its object, reminiscent of a "good" form or *Gestalt*. Nor is it entirely by chance that Freud, in introducing narcissism as subsequent to autoerotism, describes the need for *eine neue psychische Aktion, um den Narzissmus zu gestalten*—"a new psychical action to bring about narcissism."[101] Narcissism is precisely a *Gestaltung*—a giving of form to autoerotism that brings about a profound mutation in that its

---

101 "On Narcissism," SE XIV, p. 77.

action, its precipitation or coagulation, *binds* sexuality.

My schematic Model III is provisional, using arrows once again, this time to indicate that there is something like a "mirror" between ego and object—a mirror (as I have stressed elsewhere) that is not the actual device we call a mirror—the reflecting surface per se; there can be a mirror, so to speak, without a mirror.

This view of the whole, of that which totalizes—in short, of the ego—and of the object as a whole object, is constructed in the first place on the basis of Model I, which supplies its perceptions, its *Gestalten*. In fact it is by virtue of perception, and as much by virtue of the self-perception of the body (notably the body's surface) as through the perception of the other as whole—in other words by virtue of something that takes place on the level of self-preservation and its perceptual bodily functions—that the ego is gradually "formed" through successive precipitations.

The model of the whole, Model III, is constructed, then, on the basis of Model I, but also—and above all—on the basis of Model II, for Freud tells us, justifiably, that the ego draws its drive-energy from the erotic; that it is "invested" by libido, by the sexual drive, so much so that it becomes what at this moment he calls a "great reservoir of libido." This phrase would later—mistakenly—be placed in doubt by Freud. But at this juncture the idea is unambiguous: the ego is considered to be a reservoir of libido in the sense that it gets *filled*; it is not a primal reservoir, not a full tank in place from the very beginning (after the fashion of Freud's later characterization of the "id"), but a reservoir that is filled with something from outside itself, from a *source* that is precisely sexuality, and that is able subsequently to redistribute its "water" to various locations.

Model III is my representation of a kind of equilibrium described in 1914 in "On Narcissism," an unstable balance maintained by a single thread, or perhaps better by a single peg, as with a wooden framework the removal of a single peg from which has a domino effect that brings the whole structure tumbling down.

The text of 1914: an unstable equilibrium

What, then, is the peg on which this equilibrium depends? The answer is Model II. So long as the specificity of this model is not perceived, and asserted, everything is in danger of collapse. This specificity may be described from many points of view, but let me once more stress two: essence and genesis. The model is specific in its *essence* in that it is inseparable from fantasy and from the constitution of fantasy. And it is specific in its *genesis* in that it cannot be detached from the moment of seduction that constitutes it—seduction, that is, and all that occurs in seduction's wake, notably repression.

This unstable equilibrium was fated shortly to collapse. Cartoon-fashion, one model would gobble up or absorb the other two. The gobbler was to be III, the last to appear, which would devour first Model I and then—though with greater difficulty, and not uneventfully—Model II.

To use a different image, two theoretical reductions threatened to undermine and demolish this edifice. They are both mentioned as possibilities by Freud in the first pages of "On Narcissism." Before proceeding with this very important text, he notes that he must immediately confront two objections; in a way, he is foreseeing here what will happen later. The fact is that these two objections are lethal for the stability of the whole structure.

Let me quote the crucial passage, with my comments in brackets. (It was probably not by chance that "On Narcissism" was the first of Freud's writings that I translated into French.) "Before going any further I must touch on two questions which lead us to the heart of the difficulties of our subject. In the first place, what is the relation of the narcissism of which we are now speaking to auto-erotism, which we have described as an early state of the libido? [In other words, is there any good reason to distinguish between Model II and Model III?] Secondly, if we grant the ego a primary cathexis [investment] of libido, why is there any necessity for further distinguishing a sexual libido from a non-sexual energy of the ego-[drives]? Would not the postulation of a single kind of psychical energy save us all the difficulties of differentiating an energy of the ego-[drives] from ego-libido [i.e., Model I from Model II] . . .?"[102]

This devouring of theory by itself (or more precisely by narcissism), these two retreats by Freud, are none of my invention: they are there, quite clearly indicated in Freud's text.

Of the two issues it is the second, the relationship between narcissistic sexuality and self-preservation, that Freud deals with at greater length, in three awkward pages, whereas the first difficulty he summarily dismisses in the short paragraph I quoted earlier (see page 85 above).

Sexuality in danger? An awkward discussion with Jung

On the main retreat, from the sexual to the nonsexual, Freud gives us three pages in direct response to Jung. He begins as follows: "To be asked to give a definite answer to the second question . . . ".[103] The questioner is Jung, who wants to know why a distinction must be maintained between narcissistic libido and psychic energy in general. If you read these pages, which are of great historical interest, you will see how badly stuck Freud gets with this issue, offering no more than a provisional conclusion, for he leaves Jung's argument dangling and writes that Jung will be vindicated if he, Freud, is unable to prove himself right (with regard to the crucial example of schizophrenia).

The core of the matter is simple, by no means abstract, and essential to psychoanalysis. If the ego is indeed the great reservoir of libido; if all our actions ultimately pass through our love of self; if everything human beings do, supposedly to preserve their life, succeeds only inasmuch as they preserve it for the love of—of what?— for

---

102 Ibid., p. 76.
103 Ibid., p. 77.

the love of the other and for the love of themselves; if, in other words, the human being lives solely by virtue of love, then why must we insist on the existence of a level of pure self-preservation on which, in the abstract, the subject keeps himself alive with no need of love?

In the end the question is quite straightforward, but Freud's argumentation is tortuous and fragile for the simple reason that he misses the main point, which is the articulation of Models I and III. To begin with, his reasoning is clinical: psychic conflict requires that something should stand opposed to sexuality or be threatened by it. A defining feature of psychic conflict is that sexuality is contested, and repressed. But in the name of what? The question is left open. Is it self-preservation, which is to say the maintenance of our life, that is placed in danger by sexual desire? Freud adopted this position on occasion, but was never able to sustain it. Is it then perhaps the ego that sexuality threatens? If so, if the ego is the other pole of psychic conflict, we need nothing more to account for that conflict than the relationship between Models II and III, because the role of Model I is thoroughly usurped and thoroughly represented by Model III.

But over and above this reflection on the plane of the treatment and etiology of the neuroses,[104] Freud resorts (already, but also again) to arguments that he may call biological but that are really *meta*biological or even mythological. For instance: (1) Sooner or later we will succeed in isolating the sexual "substance," and for that reason we must retain the distinction between sexuality and self-preservation. (2) The fact that every living being has two cellular lineages, that of the germ-plasm and that of the soma (and here we are in the wildest kind of biological speculation), implies the reciprocal independence of sexuality (preservation of the species) and preservation of the individual. (3) Finally—last but not least—there is the com-

---

104 A train of thought that he considered secondary: "I should like at this point expressly to admit that the hypothesis of separate ego-[drives] and sexual [drives] . . . rests scarcely at all upon a psychological basis, but derives its principal support from biology" (ibid., p. 79).

mon, popular distinction between hunger and love.[105] I say last but not least because, for all the weight attached here to a "great" popular distinction (favored too by Schiller and the Romantics), Freud readily jettisoned this dichotomy in favor, as we know, of another, namely that between "love and hate." He traded one poet-philosopher for another: Schiller for Empedocles. After all, you can always find some such grand polarity and use it as a title for your theory!

I said that these arguments of Freud's were fragile, and sure enough they were soon to crumble. Once the storm had passed, he revisited their development in an encyclopedia article of 1923 entitled "The Libido Theory."[106] I propose to look briefly at three paragraphs of this short article, headed "Narcissism," "Apparent Approach to Jung's Views," and, a little further on, "Recognition of Two Classes of [Drives] in Mental Life."

Threat of Jungian monism:
reduction of self-preservation to a pansexualism . . .

The "apparent approach to Jung's views" refers, in our terms, to the absorption of Model I by Model III—the absorption of self-preservation by narcissistic Eros. To borrow a term of Freud's, this is the whole problem of "pansexualism." To state my own view right away, let me say that pansexualism, before being a theory, is a reality. Real pansexualism is something that exists before it is conceptualized and reflected on as such. It lies in the fact that in human beings sexuality is everywhere; to be more exact, it is not *immediately* everywhere, but it invades everything. This sexuality is a campaign of conquest (like all "pan-" movements, Pan-Slavism for example). Real pansexualism is a movement of conquest whereby narcissistic sexuality co-opts or usurps the functions of self-preservation. Pansexualism

---

105 Ibid., p. 78.
106 "The Libido Theory," SE XVIII, pp. 255–259.

in the realm of theory—which is what caused Freud to come close briefly to Jung's view—is nothing but the distorted reflection of real pansexualism. Such theoretical pansexualism would shortly lead to a sort of "pan-psychoanalyticism," meaning that psychoanalysis, on the basis of both real and theoretical pansexualism, ends up seeking to infiltrate related sciences, chiefly psychology, but also biology, of which it claims to be the core and essence. I note this expansionist tendency here merely to show its raison d'être, not to deplore it—for how, while saying no more, can one deplore something that has such a real foundation?

Let me quote a couple of passages from "The Libido Theory" (my comments in brackets).[107] The first is from the paragraph headed "Narcissism": "It thus turned out to be possible for object-libido to change into [investment] of the ego and *vice versa*. Further reflection showed that this process must be presumed to occur on the largest scale and that the ego is to be regarded as a great reservoir of libido from which libido is sent out *to* objects and which is always ready to absorb libido flowing back *from* objects. [An extraordinary hydraulic image! And now the point where everything shifts:] Thus the self-preservation [drives] were also of a libidinal nature [with the word 'thus' the absorption is complete]: they were sexual [drives] which, instead of external objects, had taken the subject's own ego as an object."

The self-preservation drives, therefore, are now viewed as nothing more than activity spurred by love for the ego.

And here are a few lines from the following paragraph, headed "Apparent Approach to Jung's Views": "It thus seemed on the face of it as though the slow process of psycho-analytic research was following in the steps of Jung's speculation about a primal libido, especially because the transformation of object-libido into narcissism necessarily carried along with it a certain degree of desexualization, or abandonment of the specifically sexual aims."

---

107 Ibid., p. 257.

... and reduction of pansexualism to desexualization

You will have spotted the emergence of our second problem here, the danger of Model II being absorbed by Model III. The paradox can be framed as follows. In one sense pansexualism may be said to pose no danger, internally, to our practice. We might even say that pansexualism is not merely a tendency in reality but also the tendency of psychoanalytic practice itself, which deals by definition only with sexual conflict and which reduces everything to the sexual; and this inasmuch as the sexual reduces everything in the human being to itself. So in addition to real pansexualism and theoretical pansexualism, there is a third form, namely the methodological pansexualism of psychoanalytic treatment. The psychoanalytic method is concerned solely with what it has access to, namely internal conflict on the sexual level, and the impact of such intrasexual conflict on another level, that of self-preservation, is not directly accessible to it. But it needs to be said that even though this methodological pansexualism may well characterize psychoanalytic practice,[108] its heedless transfer into the theoretical realm is fraught with danger. The danger is desexualization. To put it bluntly, if everything is sexual, then nothing is sexual. The term "sexual" loses all its force. This at bottom is what Jung played on: one can call sexual energy libido, but why not call it simply psychic energy? Others at the time argued similarly: what was referred to as psychic energy in order not to startle plain folk could always be described, in more scholarly fashion, as libido, but in any case none of this had much to do with sexuality. Nor should we forget, either, that Freud himself, as we have noted, stated that "a certain degree of desexualization, or abandonment of the specifically

---

108 And quite justifiably so: I am in no way criticizing psychoanalytic practice; what is involved here is what I have called in another context the "psychoanalytic tub," which consists precisely in this kind of reduction to sexual conflict, precisely in the subsumption of self-preservation by sexuality. See *Problématiques V: Le baquet. Transcendance du transfert* (The Tub: Transcending the Transference) (Paris: PUF, 1987).

sexual aims" was inevitably linked to narcissism in the context of an ego-based sexuality that was itself adaptive.

Nor did this danger disappear with Jung. The tendency that leads from self-preservation to pansexualism, and from pansexualism to the desexualization of analysis, is quite evident in psychoanalysis today. One has merely to consider so-called object relations theory and practice. To bring everything down to relationships with the object means banning a word, and that word is sexuality. We can, of course, speak of sexual or libidinal object relationships, but this changes almost nothing.

The absorption of Model I by Model III is thus rendered even more dangerous by the fact that II is in its turn at risk of absorption by III. Sexuality as initially described by Freud was specifically bound to fantasy; it operated in the mode of the primary processes; it was governed by the kind of associations that cause the hysteric to be overcome by anxiety or to burst into tears at the sight of a perfectly mundane object; and it was characterized by all the displacements and condensations that Freud revealed as basic to it, along with the originality of its aims, its tendency toward absolute orgasmic pleasure, and so on. But all this was then forgotten for a time, as sexuality was demoted to the status of biological functioning, goal-directed and totalizing.

Portents of desexualization

Let me note a few harbingers of this absorption of Model II by Model III.

The displacement of narcissism. Narcissism became an initial biological stage, which brings us back to the other aspect of Freud's going-astray, namely the attempt to characterize the emergence of the human being as an endogenous process. Narcissism was thrust back into the purely biological sphere and viewed as a real beginning state. Furthermore—and this is the core of the revision—what had hitherto been called autoerotism was now subordinated to this initial narcissism. Here is a passage I have quoted elsewhere from "[Drives] and Their Vicissitudes" concerning the reduction, effected in a single year (1914–1915), of autoerotism to narcissism, and thus of Model II to Model III: "Originally, at the very beginning of mental life, the ego is [invested by drives] and is to some extent capable of satisfying them on itself. We call this condition 'narcissism' and this way of obtaining satisfaction 'auto-erotic.'"[109]

Autoerotism becomes simply the type of satisfaction characteristic of the original narcissistic phase. Why? What was it that did not work about autoerotism as first conceived? What made it impossible to maintain it as an independent stage? The answer is the *setting aside of fantasy* as constitutive of autoerotism. From the instant Freud rejected the idea that autoerotism is founded on a fantasy as early as the suckling's first sexual activity, the reduction of autoerotism was already under way.

Another harbinger was *the appearance of "Eros" as synonymous with love*: a term destined, despite the semantic overlap, to dethrone, encompass, and eventually destroy the "erotic" in the name of wholeness. Love for the whole ego and love for the whole object.

Yet another sign (they are all expressions of the same tendency) is the introduction of the "life drive"—an extraordinary invention designed to denote sexuality while desexualizing it.

This reduction of sexuality to its totalizing form, to its manifestation as love, is reasserted in numerous Freudian texts, from *Beyond the Pleasure Principle* (1920) to "An Outline of Psycho-Analysis" (1938). As examples of Freud's placing Eros clearly and solely on the side of the binding function—bringing all sexuality under the heading of Model III—let me quote two passages chosen quite randomly. First, from a note to *Beyond the Pleasure Principle* (my comments in brackets):

---

[109] "Instincts and Their Vicissitudes," SE XIV, p. 134.

With the hypothesis of narcissistic libido and the extension of the concept of libido to the individual cells [speculation thus extending to the biological, cellular level], the sexual [drive] was transformed for us into Eros [in fact it is due to the establishment of narcissism that sexuality is transformed into Eros, as could not be more clearly stated], which seeks to force together and hold together the portions of living substance. What are commonly called the sexual [drives] are looked upon by us as the part of Eros which is directed towards objects.[110] [Granted, there is more than narcissism here, but this Eros directed towards objects is no less totalizing for that; Model III still rules: object-love, we might say, is a projected narcissism.]

Here is the beginning of my second passage, from "An Outline of Psycho-Analysis": "The aim of [Eros] . . . is to establish ever greater unities and to preserve them thus—in short, to bind together."[111]

Are we to assume, then, that sexuality had gone over entirely, bag and baggage, to the function of binding? Model III, having gobbled up Model I, was on the verge of swallowing Model II. Pansexualism had become pan-Eros, or pan-love; and on the far side of this pan-Eros loomed a kind of pan-vitalism. Consider, for example, the reference to "living substance" down to the cellular level. As noted earlier in this course, Aristophanes' myth, cited in *Three Essays* as an old wives' tale, now emerged, thanks to an extraordinary and magical metamorphosis, as the very paradigm of sexuality. Fast disappearing were the partitioned, perverse, and goal-less sexuality described in *Three Essays* (and again in some sense in "[Drives] and Their Vicissitudes"), the role of fantasy, and the role of the repressed unconscious at the origins of the drive.

---

110 SE XVIII, pp. 60–61n.
111 SE XXIII, p. 148.

The death drive to the rescue. Life and Death in Psychoanalysis

But then, happily, what Aristotle calls a peripeteia occurred: a reversal, or at least a partial one, indicated that erotic sexuality would not allow itself to be swallowed in this way, for its radical, unbound aspect had to re-emerge somewhere. It was indeed impossible for Freud to have simply forgotten his discovery, and sexuality was bound to survive the catastrophe somehow. So here is the remainder of my quotation from the "Outline": "the aim of the [other drive, the antagonist of Eros] is, on the contrary, to undo connections and so to destroy things."[112] And here we have the resurgence—the reappearance at another place—of what it has not been possible for narcissistic Eros to encompass: of something which, as we all know, is called the death drive.

"Why the Death Drive?" is the title of the long final chapter of my *Life and Death in Psychoanalysis,* to which I can do no better than refer you: I re-read it last night and, aside from a few misprints, could find nothing to challenge in it. In particular, this chapter should enable you to read *Beyond the Pleasure Principle* (1920) in another way. For such a re-reading I suggest the following framework: in the first place, if sexuality is nothing more than a totalizing Eros, and if this sexuality functions according to a pleasure principle conceived of as a principle of homeostasis, of stability, then a "beyond the pleasure principle" is needed precisely because a "beyond"—or a "prior to"—is needed for that totalizing Eros. I say "prior to" in order to reassert the existence of something that may be considered, logically speaking, more primary—in the sense of the primary process—than binding (even if binding and unbinding complement each other). The death drive is thus the reaffirmation of an unbinding force that psychoanalysis posited from the start in its very methodology and in its approach to unconscious processes: the unbinding force at work

---

112 Ibid.

in what is called the primary process.

Second (following the three points enumerated in *Life and Death*), the death drive reaffirms the priority of the reflexive or "self-" phase in the development of the drive.[113] This reflexive phase (I would now add) should be viewed as directly related to the process of metabolization and repression.

Third, and last, the death drive reaffirms the idea of an attack from within by a foreign body introduced into the individual's psychic apparatus: this "self-aggression" is the deepest meaning of what is called the death drive.

For today, however, I want to make three critical remarks about this concept (or supposed concept): (1) the death drive lacks characteristics essential for the restorations for which it strives; (2) the death drive transposes the conflict onto a "meta"-plane; (3) the death drive makes it possible to conceal contraband.

(1) The unvarnished concept of the death drive lacks essential features. If you have followed my argument you will appreciate that the very foundation of my thesis, namely seduction, is absent; the same goes for fantasy as source of the drive, and for the process of repression as generator of fantasy. A death drive without repression, that does not even have its roots in the process of repression, is devoid of what in my view constitutes the essential aspect of the genesis of drives in the human being, namely the "demonic" character that the death drive is nonetheless supposed to reaffirm.

(2) The transfer of psychic conflict onto a meta-plane amounts to the relegation of the entire inquiry, which initially hewed closely to direct experience, to speculation that could be described as metaphysical or, perhaps even more accurately, as metabiological: speculation about the origins of life, about the evolution of living organisms, about the distinction between germ-plasm and soma—speculation too that

---

113 See my discussion of the three recurring elements that propel the introduction of the death drive in *Life and Death in Psychoanalysis*, pp. 112ff.

does not shrink from seeking models in the myth of Aristophanes or among the pre-Socratic philosophers. The terms "life" and "death" themselves can hardly be considered biological: any biological science could easily dispense with them. Freud introduces them into his account of sexual conflict, where they have no place, save, I would say, in a more than metaphorical way that is profoundly inappropriate. All this metabiological speculation bespeaks the return in force of the problem of the *Zweck*, of goal-directedness—of a purposefulness of sexuality that Freud now seeks to show is present from the start in the form of the repetition compulsion.[114] In other words, we may say that the two great modes of functioning of sexuality, in accordance with two principles of mental functioning—not the pleasure and reality principles, but rather the principles of binding and unbinding—are now considered to be drives or indeed, as I would go so far as to say, to be *instincts*. Admittedly, Freud continues to use the word *Trieb* to refer to the life drives (*Lebenstriebe*) and the death drive (*Todestrieb*)—with the former usually in the plural and the latter in the singular—but in actuality everything suggests that what we have here is a return of *Instinkt*; indeed, *Beyond the Pleasure Principle* includes an explicit discussion of instinctual behavior in the shape of an appreciative evocation of the great migrations of animals, of fish traveling upstream to spawn, or the flights of birds of passage—return journeys spurred by instinct, by something that is unquestionably a *Zweck*.[115]

A few goings-astray with the death drive

(3) My third point concerning the unfortunate inadequacy, even fallaciousness, of the backtracking implied by the introduction of the death drive, is that the invention of the term itself, with all its lack of precision and all its romanticism, facilitated the smuggling in

---

114 See above, p. 17 and pp. 32–33, n. 42
115 SE XVIII, pp. 36–37.

of a great variety of things, some of them far from desirable. How many times thereafter did psychoanalysts find themselves under strict orders from "philosophy" not to forget the death drive, which made such fine speculations possible? This wondrous term can cover practically anything. For some it implies a striving for Nirvana, something extremely peaceful, a kind of latent Buddhism or utterly pacific and unruffled transcendental meditation; according to others, however, it means something close to Dionysian frenzy. Leaning toward the frenzy view, Freud allowed himself to speak of a "pure culture of the death [drive]"[116]—one can almost picture swarms of frantic bacteria or destructive viruses under the microscope. By contrast, and at other moments, it is absolute silence that characterizes a death drive under whose sway nothing "makes waves."

Here is another example. The real problem of aggression was to be covered up definitively, or at least for a very long time, by the death drive, which clearly offered nothing but the most abstract solution to that problem. A solution, moreover, that is barely discernible, strange to say, in *Beyond the Pleasure Principle*, where aggression is hardly mentioned. In any case, the notion of the death drive has since become an all-purpose device—a skeleton key—used with abandon and in any way possible to avoid dealing with the highly complex mechanisms in play in aggression. Those mechanisms need to be completely revisited so as to disentangle them on the basis of the three levels mentioned earlier: the vital and animal, the erotic, and the narcissistic (see Figure 5, page 93 above). Instead, the death drive has served to prevent any such clarification.

Yet another instance of the shortcomings of the notion of the death drive is its unreserved conflation with a wish for biological death. This is a simple verbal trick that facilitates an effortless attribution of any bodily process resulting in death to a supposedly primary factor. In practical terms, not a year goes by for me, as a director of

116 *The Ego and the Id* (1923), SE XIX, p. 53.

research, without my being asked to supervise some project—on cancer, for instance—in which the death drive is immediately evoked. The existentialists' "being-for-death" is likewise liable to be smuggled in under the cloak of the death drive, with which it was naturally identified very early on: here at long last was something in psychoanalysis that harmonized with metaphysical ambitions! Even Lacan joined the campaign for being-for-death under the banner of the death drive.

Despite all this "covering-up," consistent with the fact that the death drive is arguably nothing but a "cover formation" (*Deckbildung*), Freud at least drew the line when it came to being-for-death), and this notwithstanding his personal, pathos-laden relationship to death—the death of his intimates as well as his own. He held fast to the view that there is no such idea as death in the unconscious (a statement of scant consequence, however, if one accepts that there are quite simply *no* ideas in the unconscious[117]); but Freud also stated, hewing closer to experience and observation, that the conscious idea of death is not *primary*, that it is acquired by the child, in a concrete manner, in the individual's history, that it is similarly acquired in the history of the species (see *Totem and Taboo* [1912–1913] and other writings), and furthermore that its acquisition is mediated by the death of others, whether by the loss or, as sometimes happens, the murder of another. The tragic aspect of the idea of death is not diminished by saying that the idea is acquired and mediated by the death of the other.

As I mentioned earlier, the last chapter of my *Life and Death in Psychoanalysis* is titled "Why the Death Drive?" It is worth reading this question in two ways: Why the death drive *in Freud*? And why keep the death drive *after* Freud?

I have passed Freud's conception of the death drive in review several times in order to point up its chief function as a resurgence and a rebalancing factor, but also as a means of concealment. In order

---

117 No idea of "life" either, for that matter.

to preserve the word "death" in this context, we find ourselves continually obliged to qualify it: to speak of a "death drive for the ego," or—and above all—to defend its use solely in terms of a "sexual death drive," a drive of sexual unbinding.

But can we go on following in Freud's footsteps here ad infinitum? Has not the term, the signifier, "death drive" attained an intrinsic weight sufficient to render vain any further development of the idea? What is more, has not this weight become a threat to psychoanalytic thinking—an actual inhibitor of thought?

Freud's straying towards biology culminates in the dichotomy between the life and death drives. Little wonder that this deviation should solidify within the psychoanalytical tendency that took this dichotomy the most seriously, while reframing it as an opposition between sexuality and aggression. I am referring of course to the school of Melanie Klein.

All that has been lost by Kleinianism

I have already mentioned several ways in which Kleinian theory and Kleinian practice forget Freud's main discoveries. Let me return to a few of them. Ultimately they are all interconnected.

The Kleinians abandon the Freudian method precisely inasmuch as it enshrines the etymological sense of "analysis" (unloosening), or in other words its submission to the primary process. They replace that method by a hermeneutics, reverting to an interventional mode that is pre-Freudian, though in a new guise. Their means of interpretation becomes the theoretical grid itself: the principles of binding and unbinding, now dubbed love and hate, are pressed into service as all-purpose interpretive tools crammed, as it were, into the patient's head. This has already been well described by Maurice Dayan in an article entitled "Mrs. K. interpreted,"[118] but what I want

---

118 "Mme K... interpréta," in Maurice Dayan, *L'arbre des styles* (Paris: Aubier-Montaiagne, 1980, pp. 107–163).

to add is that this is a masked return to the old "hermeneutics."

Another major loss entailed by Kleinian theory is the reference to self-preservation. I pointed out earlier that such a loss is not in itself critical for psychoanalysis, since the proper work of psychoanalytic practice takes place on Models II and III of our scheme, with the "psychoanalytic tub" effecting precisely this sort of abstraction of—or caesura with—self-preservation. But this does not mean that self-preservation does not exist, or that it cannot be referred to when we wish to describe the nature of psychoanalysis (and of sexuality) with respect to human beings. Paradoxically, Melanie Klein herself works exclusively on Models II and III, which is to say in the realm proper to psychoanalysis, but for her these levels become so to speak phantasmagorical, the site of combat between mystical entities— good and bad, love and aggression, whole and part. Mythical entities, then—but also biological ones, for all development of fantasy, and even its very genesis, are conceived of by her in terms of endogeny. These are in fact great "instincts," dominating the combat and finding expression in the individual only in retail form.

What is more, what ultimately loses any real place with the antagonistic pairing of love and aggression is sexuality. As with the Freudian conception of Eros, the sexual becomes totalizing, synthesizing love. As for unbound and unbinding sexuality, it takes every ounce of good will on our part to discern it at work tucked away in the Kleinian system, lurking behind the mask of destructiveness, as for example in the paranoid position or in the bad, aggressive part-object.

This considerable shift of perspective is reflected on the metapsychological plane. Obviously the idea of leaning-on, for instance, no longer has any place: the drives have absolutely always existed, so that the development of sexuality in the individual is quite unproblematic. Seduction, with its necessary foundation, the priority of the other in the constitution of a sexual subject, is likewise perfectly alien to a system in which the adult-as-object serves above all as a point of purchase for instinctual tendencies that are by their nature endogenous in children.

Lastly, it must be said, apropos of the most classical of meta-psychological concepts, the problematic of repression and that of the unconscious as a separate sphere with its own laws and contents, that these are the very least of the concerns of a school of thought that unreservedly espoused an alternative Freudian formulation according to which everything that is conscious was once unconscious. To restate my question: What are we to do with the death drive after Freud? Within a coherent system like Kleinianism, it functions as a thoroughly integrated element within a biologizing or metabiologizing makeover of psychoanalysis. Among many present-day authors it serves as a kind of spare part used on a case-by-case basis when there is a need to mitigate a variety of difficulties and impasses arising in clinical practice.

A new foundation for psychoanalysis: retrieving Freudian "exigency"

In the context of a systematic refoundation of psychoanalysis—and once its conjunctural role in the Freudian edifice has been well understood—the death drive will probably seem to us a superfluous idea when it comes to defining the players and stakes in mental conflict.

II

Biologism and Biology

Lecture given on October 23, 1997,
at the University of Buenos Aires on the occasion of
the author's reception of an honorary doctorate.

Psychoanalysis and Biology: Realities and Ideologies

The question I propose to tackle today is timely. It is also vast. I will try to bring something new to the issue by not framing it mainly on the naively realistic level of the relationship between two supposedly competing disciplines, as for example, "Is psychoanalysis related to biology?" or "Does biology confirm or invalidate the discoveries of psychoanalysis, and does it render the practice of psychoanalysis obsolete?" Instead I will attempt to reverse the question: "What is the function, well before modern biology, of references to the living world in the constitution of the human subject?"

Before getting that far, however, let me outline my position on two issues that I address not as a specialist but merely as an educated person, or perhaps as a philosopher: (1) the supposed utility of a dialogue between psychoanalysis and modern biology, neurobiology, and neurophysiology; and (2) the special and quite peculiar relationship of psychoanalysis to genetics.

I

With regard to the first question, the issue of a dialogue between biology and psychoanalysis, let me state matters this way. My starting point is materialist. The proposition that there can be no thought without corresponding bodily changes seems to me incontrovertible. Immense as the advances of modern biology have been, it does not seem to me that they have shaken this principle, which was espoused by Spinoza and well before him by the entire materialist tradition of Antiquity. A certain number of reservations are nevertheless in order in this regard. In the first place, we should note that we are getting further and further from the idea of a one-to-one correspondence between a given localized process in the nervous system and a given circumscribed mental process. I do not believe that the neurophysiologist can justifiably expect, even at some indefinite future time, to identify the mathematical distinction between quadratic and cubic equations in a given localized process in the brain; and this notwithstanding the obvious fact that such cerebral processes are material in nature, as is demonstrated beyond doubt by the effect of drugs, say, on a mathematician's thinking. It is clear that we have not, and no doubt never will, discover a drug that interferes with quadratic equations without affecting cubic ones.

I have just used the phrase "at some indefinite future time." Most discussions of biology's relationship to mental processes assume that this is not yet known. Without doubt, of course, our understanding of nature has no limits. Science's "not yet" counters the notion of a closed system of knowledge. But in the specific case that concerns us here, I think that something else is involved—another, more indispensable *"not yet."* Being able to say "We do *not yet* know what cerebral processes are the basis of scientific reasoning" is a vital necessity. The "not yet" here is an *absolute*. Were it otherwise, a researcher writing a paper in neurobiology would have to accept that his own reasoning at this precise moment has no claim, in relative terms, to any consistency of its own.

Let me explain: if, miraculously, biological research ever managed to account for every thought process in physical terms, the biologist would have no further questions to answer. His interlocutors would be convinced by purely material means. This speculation plunges us, however, into an abyssal perplexity: are we to suppose, say, that one day the content of an article in a neuroscientific journal could be injected like a neuroleptic drug?

116

I have not yet mentioned psychoanalysis, which for my part I see as no more and no less closely related to neurobiological processes than is aesthetics, say, or logic, or the reasoning of the physicist. The fact is that the order of thought constitutes a whole, just as the material order does. There is no mental process of which it may be said that it is more dependent than some other one on its material underpinning.

So the question arises, why pick psychoanalysis? Why are we perpetually asking whether biological discoveries will eventually dethrone psychoanalysis? The question is essentially as foolish as asking whether advances in biology will dethrone mathematics or logic.

Why psychoanalysis? Why should it be considered a privileged interlocutor for biology? I can see only one major reason for this, and it is not objective but subjective: if the neurosciences ever realized their project (despite the "not yet"), they would explain everything, including the development and mechanics of the neurosciences themselves, along with the thought processes of biologists. Whence the necessity of placing constraints on the *unthinkable* idea of physical determinism applying to the workings of the scientist's own thinking.

The easiest constraint derives from the distinction between normal and pathological, giving rise to two parallel claims, namely (1) that psychoanalysis is exclusively concerned with the pathological, and (2) that neurobiology is more at home with descriptions of psychopathology than with descriptions of normal phenomena. This twofold claim is very convenient, but it is false. False with regard to psychoanalysis, which has little interest in the normal/pathological distinction. The psychoanalytic notion of psychic conflict is universal in its application. False too with regard to neurobiology, which cannot shrink from studying all mental processes, be they normal or pathological, cognitive or affective.

The renewed quest for so-called dialogue is promoted by neurobiology rather than by psychoanalysis, or rather, more precisely, by specialized journalists stimulated by incessant and noisy declarations from researchers. To my mind this is a way for biology to avoid confronting the theoretically boundless, and strictly speaking "abyssal" nature of its own research—and to do so by attacking what it construes as the weakest link in the chain of the human sciences.

For myself, I invariably subsume this whole debate under the more general rubric of the opposition between biology and the sciences of man as a whole, a sphere where psychoanalysis has no special status.

II

I come now to another aspect of the subject that should not be conflated with the one just discussed. I am referring to the *genetic* perspective. Modern genetics reframes in new terms the old contrast between *innate* and *acquired*, an antagonism that psychoanalysis, and Freud, quite rightly never sought to evade. As futile as it is to be continually bringing up the philosophical question of mind versus body, nothing could be more important, for our practice as for our theory, than a clear idea of what is known as (individual) acquisition.

Let me put the enormous advances of present-day genetics into a few words intelligible to the nonspecialist: the discovery and identification of genes, their artificial modification and their transplantation, and the production of a sort of map of the genome.

A remarkable achievement, even if there a still a long way to go. But what exactly is inscribed in genes? In each gene? Consider for example the production of a hormone. Or the development of a part of the body. A recent conference of geneticists clearly reined in the ambitions, one might even say the fantasies, of partisans of the idea that "everything is genetic" (rather like the claim that "everything is electrical").[119] To borrow an example from medicine, diabetes is partly

---

119 Dijon, September 1997. See the contribution of Bertrand Jordan: "La 'Chasse aux gènes', quelques enjeux et conséquences" (The "Hunt for Genes": Some Stakes and Consequences).

a familial illness, but there is no such thing as a gene for diabetes. A number of genes are implicated, located at different points, and in any case the genetic factor is only one of several determinants of this condition, environmental influences being cardinal.

In our own area, manic depression is a familial illness with which no single gene has as yet been matched. Regarding homosexuality, scientific journals once mistakenly claimed that a corresponding gene had been isolated, and I will not revisit the socio-psychological controversy that this precipitated. The "everything is genetic" craze has even gone so far as to try to identify a gene for "criminality."

The fact is that genes seem to have only a limited, partial impact in time and space, for they are necessarily involved in a multifactorial reality. Nor do they in themselves constitute a stable structure, their triggering often being sequential.

Let me recall a small event a while back involving cloning experiments. The great fear then was that identical individuals with precisely the same genetic heredity might one day be manufactured on an industrial basis—on a conveyor belt as it were. Renowned geneticists were obliged to intervene in the media-driven debate and point out that such identical individuals already exist in the shape of homozygous twins, and that we know from experience that their existence and destiny can unfold in quite different ways.

How is psychoanalysis positioned relative to this vast progress in genetics?

It must be said that, along with Freud himself, it is very badly positioned. Let me briefly recall that Freud returned to the hereditary hypothesis when he abandoned the seduction theory. He did so by appealing to phylogenesis. Having discovered the full scope of sexuality's bond with fantasy, especially with regard to *childhood* sexuality, he was obliged to trace this association to its origin, to its acquisition. This was necessarily either interpersonal in character—as per the seduction theory—or else genetic (though this was well before the discoveries of genetics; in those days one used the terms "hereditary" or "atavistic"). In 1897 Freud abandoned the seduction theory and rallied definitively to the second thesis: "the factor of a hereditary disposition regains a sphere of influence from which I had made it my task to dislodge it."[120]

This was what is known as the phylogenetic hypothesis. The term itself already embodies a distortion, because "phylum" is understood by genetics as a succession of species, whereas Freud restricted its meaning to the human species, formulating detailed hypotheses on the history or prehistory of the process of acquisition. In his account, fantasy scenes experienced in the present had been imprinted by real prehistorical experiences common to the species and often repeated. This is, of course, an hypothesis more Lamarckian than Darwinian.

For Freud phylogenesis is the theoretical explanation for the "primal fantasies": castration, the witnessing of parental coitus (primal scene), seduction, and so on. These grand hypotheses concerning prehistory and fantasy are set forth in *Totem and Taboo* and *Moses and Monotheism,* works that carry the thesis as far as it will go, upholding the notion of a genetic inscription of the murder of the father, and thus ultimately of the Oedipus complex.

Let me state flatly, based on what modern genetics has taught us, that the idea of a scene, scenario, or fantasy with a historical content such as the murder of the father being inscribed on any specific gene as a representation is strictly impossible. Let me say too, apropos of the supposed mechanism of inscription, that the acceptance of Darwinism, or modern neo-Darwinism, makes it inconceivable that a prehistoric scene, no matter how many times repeated, could eventually be imprinted and transmitted in the form of a fantasy.

In short, psychoanalysis was led into an impasse by the idea of phylogenesis. But fortunately this did not mean that it was finished with the question of innate structures.

As we know, psychoanalysis—particularly French psycho-

---

120 Freud to Fliess, September 21, 1897. *Letters to Fliess*, p. 265.

120

analysis—has posited a major distinction between drive and instinct. This opposition (*Trieb/Instinkt*) is present throughout Freud's work, but James Strachey, and in his wake the entirety of English-language psychoanalysis, has confused matters by translating *Trieb* as *instinct*.

To follow Freud, we may say that *Instinkt*/instinct denotes behavior that is (1) goal-directed; (2) relatively unchanging; and (3) inherited, not acquired. Thus the mechanisms of the oral prehension of food, mastication, and swallowing may be considered instinctual.

Trieb/drive, by contrast, denotes a force that is (1) not goal-directed to begin with; (2) variable from one individual to the next; and (3) determined by the individual's history. The drive par excellence is the sexual one. Even if its presence is inevitable in a given individual, it is bound to fantasy, which for its part is strictly personal.

This distinction, while essential, is continually overlooked.

The basic concern of psychoanalysis is the drive, its acquisition, and its forms. But this is not at all to say that instinct in the human being is neglected. For one thing, we acknowledge the existence of what are called the self-preservative instincts, linked to life and survival. I just mentioned swallowing, for example. But matters extend much further than this, beyond simple primary needs. The primal relationship to the mother, which is intersubjective from the outset, is undoubtedly marked by instinct. This is true even though this relationship is as it were shot through, transfixed, by seduction.

Nor is instinct in the human being solely self-preservative. There is a sexual instinct—not only a sexual drive. We are fairly well acquainted with this phenomenon, which is bound up with the maturing of the genital organs: an essentially hormonal process, pubertal and pre-pubertal.

I must now request your full attention.

The easy path is to argue as follows: first there is the *innate*, genetic sexuality, and then comes the *acquired*: modifications, modulations, at times aberrations vis-à-vis the innate. The acquired is thus founded on the innate. What could be more logical? But all this reasoning was swept away when Freud discovered infantile, so-called *pregenital* sexuality.

(1) Although it may invest the genital organs, pregenital sexuality is by no means confined to them: it may focus on the oral or anal zone or indeed on any region of the body.

(2) It is not bound to goal-directed behavior (coitus) but rather to fantasies, and fantasies of very great variety.

(3) It is variable with respect to its aim and its object, a variability that is dealt with at length in *Three Essays on the Theory of Sexuality*.

(4) It is unattached, anarchic, and "polymorphous."

Now, nothing in the emergence and development of this infantile sexuality lends support to the idea of genetic determinism. No specific hormonal mechanism can be identified for each partial (oral or anal) sexual drive. As for the *succession* of supposed "stages," it is highly questionable from the standpoint of observation, which makes it even more problematic to seek a genetically governed sequence laid down according to a time-line.

What we are thus obliged to conclude is frankly stupefying: in human sexuality and its development the *acquired* emerges not *on the basis of* the innate, but in fact *before* the innate. This is very important, especially for the psychology of adolescence, for at the moment when instinct comes into play the field is entirely "occupied" by the drive and its underpinning, namely fantasy. Whence the notion of a junction at puberty between drive and instinct. But it must be borne in mind that whatever the genetic component in human sexuality may be, it cannot remain unmodified, as witness its immense variation in the adult individual.

I have offered an account of the genesis of drive-governed sexuality, as acquired in the child-adult relationship, under the rubric of a "general theory of seduction." I may say a little about this later, but first I want to discuss *biology as ideology*.

III

Ideology and myth are stories, usually collective, made up by humans. What is their aim? Their function? I have sought to assign them a role in my general theory of seduction.

But first let me address a question nearer to today's topic. In myths and ideologies a cardinal, central part is played by the relationship to the world of other living things, to the animal or bestial. Well before modern biology there was a spontaneous biologism. Perhaps we should call it "animalism." Before I outline the function of this kind of reference to the order of living things, let me give a few examples.

First of all, consider *totemism*. Here, very briefly, is what is meant by this term. Totemism is the attribution to a so-called primitive human group of a specific animal or, more rarely, a plant. This animal or plant is looked upon, in accordance with a foundational myth, as the ancestor of the group. The group assumes the name of the totem animal and identifies with it to a greater or lesser degree. The animal is the object of rites and, especially, of innumerable prohibitions.

The phenomenon of totemism has long fascinated ethnologists. Here I will mention two major interpretations, that of Freud and that of Claude Lévi-Strauss and other anthropologists.

In Freud's account, the totem is conflated with the father, the primal father, and bound up with the father's murder, his cult, and his incorporation (the totem meal). Totemic prohibitions are ultimately derived from the oedipal one. This theory fails to address totemism's countless variations, for it ignores the human's relationship to the animal world in general, as well as to specific animals; most important, it fails to account for the existence of totemic *systems*. It is rare to find an isolated totem; totems tend to constitute a relational system among themselves.

For his part, Lévi-Strauss takes the opposite path, and this to the point of paradox. His *Totemism* (1962)[121] represents the most extreme structuralist position, arguing that totemism is a system of classification, a "taxonomy" with a social function. Totemism is dissolved into an almost absolute nominalism.

More recently, Lévi-Strauss's thinking has evolved a good deal relative to such formalism. His analyses seek to explain why a particular animal is opposed to or allied with another one. Admittedly, the purpose is still to create order. But Lévi-Strauss goes further: in *The Jealous Potter* he suggests that myths (and totemism is implicated here) have as their function "relieving intellectual uneasiness and even existential anxiety."[122]

From our perspective, we still have to account for the universal presence of the animal realm as a point of reference for humans. Little appreciated by either Freud or Lévi-Strauss, this reference to the *beast*, to the animal as *bestia*, is indeed virtually universal. The ancient Greek worldview already placed humans midway between the bestial and the divine, while acknowledging that the gods had to assume beastly form in order to commit their heinous crimes. For the Greeks the beast is a sexual beast. Zeus takes the form of the bull or the swan to seduce his lovers. The beast is sexual, and also cruel: the Minotaur mistreats his young victims before devouring them. He is hidden in the deepest part of his den. The notion that an animal nature lies *in the deepest part of human beings* is an almost inescapable corollary. For Plato the "passions" represent the animal and bestial bedrock of our nature.

Closer to us in time there is the wolf. Hobbes's dictum, *Homo homini lupus*, is well known to us, and is intended to remind us that human beings are capable of every kind of cruelty. Elsewhere I have

---

121 *Le Totémisme aujourd'hui* (Paris: PUF, 1962); Eng. trans. by Rodney Needham: *Totemism* (Boston: Beacon Press, 1963).
122 *La Potière jalouse* (Paris: Plon, 1985), p. 227; Eng. trans. by Bénédicte Chorier: *The Jealous Potter* (Chicago: University of Chicago Press, 1988), p. 171.

tried to show how this formulation embodies an ideology.[123] The wolf, the real wolf, is cruel neither to other wolves, nor to its victims, nor to us. With very rare exceptions, cruelty has no place in an animal's nature. Yet our species has contrived a myth of animality, or bestiality, to which even Freud fell prey. The bestial so conceived is said to be our most drive-bound and cruel characteristic—and our most profound. A Leviathan.

The human is sometimes a beast, not just a living being but a depraved and sexual beast, often a cruel Leviathan, and frequently both. But this invocation of the animal world is purely ideological: it allows us to slough off our unconscious by assigning it to the nonhuman in us, to the so-called "pre-human" supposedly crouching in our depths, whereas in reality it is human beings who create this bestial nonhuman realm, this *id*, within themselves.

I cannot proceed without mentioning another example of this reference to the world of living things. I mean the "castration complex," as discovered and systematized by Freud. I should say right away that here Freud takes us for a ride through a succession of fallacies in which he himself becomes entangled. The very basis of the castration complex, the idea that the origin of the difference between the sexes stems from a removal of the penis—that the female has been castrated—is initially related to anatomy, as per the celebrated saying "anatomy is destiny." Freud elaborates on this idea by writing that "the morphological distinction is bound to find expression in differences of psychical development."[124] He refers, in other words, not to sexual physiology but to a descriptive morphology.

Even in its own terms, this appeal to an anatomico-morphological "destiny" is open to criticism, because the anatomy invoked is a *false* one, strictly visual and determined by the features of the human *habitus*. Everyone knows, in fact, with or without any acquaintance

---

123 "La soi-disant pulsion de mort: une pulsion sexuelle" (The So-Called Death Drive: A Sexual Drive), *Adolescence*, February 15, 1997, pp. 205–224.
124 "The Dissolution of the Oedipus Complex," SE XIX, p. 178.

with biological science, that female animals, just like males, have visible external genitalia. In humans, by contrast, because of our erect posture, the female's external genital organs are hidden, whence the illusion, especially in children, that they do not exist, and that the difference between the sexes is that the one is sexed and the other unsexed.

But it is here, suddenly, that this romance of a primal theory acquires the status for Freud of a scientific and irrefutable biological fact. It is in "Analysis Terminable and Interminable" (1937) that he connects the end of analysis to a confrontation with an insurmountable obstacle in both sexes, namely the rejection of castration. He even concludes that in castration he has discovered the *gewachsene Fels*, the underlying bedrock that analysis cannot penetrate. But he has no hesitation in attributing this "rock" to scientifically confirmed biological reality: "The repudiation of femininity can be nothing else than a biological fact, a part of the great riddle of sex."[125] And when Freud invokes "biology," the myth of phylogenesis is never far away.

It thus behooves us to mistrust an appeal to "biological science" that in fact relies on what I call the human being's spontaneous "animalism." Such animalism is ideology and myth. It is theory only in the sense in which Freud speaks of the "sexual theories of childhood." Millennia before the advent of biology as the science of living things, humans were making mythical, philosophical, ultimately ideological references to the order of living things, to animals, to the animal or bestial world.

What is the purpose of this proliferation of ideologies that invoke a realm of "living" things with no scientific basis at all? This is where my "general theory of seduction" can help clarify matters. In brief, this theory deals with the child's reaction to the trauma occasioned by messages from adults, usually verbal but also behavioral, that are tinged with unconscious sexuality, and that in this sense are

---

125 SE XXIII, p. 252.

enigmatic. Freud showed how two essentially "biologizing" child-hood theories were able to bind what was enigmatic: the cloacal theory and the theory of castration. Both were absolutely false, the one postulating the birth of babies through the anus, the other ascribing the difference between the sexes to castration.[126]

These theories—or ideologies—are indispensable, even if we refuse them the illusory and pompous dignity that Lacan bestows on them under the metaphysical category of "the Symbolic" (not forgetting the capital "S"!). They are translation codes made available to the child, or infant, by its cultural world—tools for interpreting, with varying success, the messages of adults. Such translation inevitably leaves traces, relics, that are not bound by symbolization precisely because they are repressed unconscious content that is itself the source of the drives. There exist, in short, certain "theories," false theories, ancient, apparently biological, that situate humans relative to the world of living things. They are intended to master not the sexual instinct but rather drive-governed sexuality, the sexual dimension that intrudes into the adult-child relationship via the seemingly innocent messages sent by the adult to the child. Totemism, the castration myth, the myth of the primal beast within us, far from being *sources* of anxiety, are thus instruments for attempting to *master* it.

It remains for me to say something about the Oedipus complex. When it proves impossible to subscribe to the prehistorical (atavistic) reality of the primal horde and the murder of the father, attempts are made to prove the "universality" of the Oedipus complex either on an anthropological basis or on a biological one.

In Lévi-Strauss's work and that of his followers, anthropology's basic framework deals with the laws of human exchange, with relationships between groups, and with unavoidable differences between the sexes and generations. When it comes to the prohibition of incest, the account proposed is naturally of the structuralist kind.

---

126 "On the Sexual Theories of Children," SE IX, pp. 209–234.

Little needs adding to such anthropological descriptions, except perhaps to say that they demonstrate how varied the systems are that structure kinship systems. A fundamental aspect of the Oedipus complex, the supposed murder of the father, is not seen here to have the the universality posited for it by Freud. As for incest, from the anthropological point of view son-mother or father-daughter incest seems to be less important than the prohibition affecting groups of brothers and sisters.

Some authors, failing to find the unique and universal oedipal schema in anthropology, have concluded that this universality is supported by modern biology. They cite the union of gametes, the model of the "double spiral," and the fusion of two genetic inheritances as the biological undergirding of the Oedipus complex, as if there were the slightest relation between the very widespread (but certainly not universal) phenomenon of sexual reproduction and the twofold prohibition on incest and parricide. It would be easy, if rather laborious, to expose the fallacies underlying this connection between the Oedipus complex and present-day biogenetics. Let me just say this: the ambition is to have Oedipus ("the man with swollen feet") walk (so to speak) on the two feet of anthropology and biology. Unfortunately, it turns out that the "biological" foot, the reference to genetics, is perfectly mythical, so one might well say that Oedipus limps because he is walking on just one foot—the anthropological one.

Well before modern genetics, humans were forever referring—and clinging—to myths about living things.

Before the birth of genetics there was, quite simply, Genesis, the first book of the Bible. It was Genesis, notably, that imposed the idea that sexual union necessarily implies the importance of a parental couple. One instance of this among others is the story of Noah. What was the nature of the disorder the Flood was supposed to rectify? I quote: "And it came to pass, when men began to multiply on the face of the earth, and daughters were born unto them, that the sons of God saw the daughters of men that they were fair, and they took them wives of all which they chose" (Gen. 6:1–2).

In other words, the threat was sexuality independent of defined couples and generational distinctions. Hence the building of Noah's ark: of all the animals "there went in two and two unto Noah into the ark, the male and the female, as God had commanded Noah" (Gen. 7:9).

This is the famous scene represented by Walt Disney, with Mr. and Mrs. Elephant, Mr. and Mrs. Snake, and—beyond all plausibility for anyone acquainted with the life of insects—Mr. and Mrs. Fly.

What I want to emphasize is the extent to which, even here, a purely mythical view of the realm of living things is used by our species as a means of ordering and binding drives—*our own drives*.

We humans can by no means escape material constraints. On the other hand, the entire history of the species is that of an emancipation from the order of living things. As though fearful of that emancipation, humans are continually situating themselves in a discourse concerning the realm of living things (a "bio-logy"), and this well before any modern biology. This bio-ideo-logical reference is still far from having said its last word. With regard to every problem confronted by humanity, it is the animal world, not mankind, that is referred to.

There is more and more talk of "bio-ethics"—as though a morality could somehow be derived from life. Even the Christian religion is now more ready to invoke the "rights of living things" than the precepts of its founder.

For the sake of clarity let me sum up what I have had to say this evening.

Biology and psychoanalysis. There is nothing specific about the exchange between these two realms relative to the eternal dialogue between the science of the physical and the science of the mental. On the other hand, we can try to dispel the misunderstandings that tend to make psychoanalysis a privileged interlocutor for the neurosciences.

Genetics and psychoanalysis. The debate here has indeed been profoundly stimulated by modern genetics, which has demolished the hopes of Freudian "phylogenesis." But the genetics of sexuality must be confronted with the following paradox, as illuminated by the general theory of seduction: in the history of the human individual, acquired sexuality precedes innate sexuality, this on account of the young human's early contact with adult sexuality.

Finally, psychoanalysis has much to say about the immemorial eagerness of humans to appeal to ideologies of the living world. It also has much to say about the mental function of these ideologies, which consists in the binding and circumscribing of a sexual drive that is originally anarchic.

Index

Aberrations, sexual, 23-25; *see also* Perversion(s)

Abraham, Karl, 26, 70-71

acquired/innate distinction, 118, 120-22; *see also* heredity

ad hoc hypotheses, 8

Adler, Alfred, 6

adult other, 4, 57-58, 62-70

agency, ego as 77-78, 81, 88

aggression, 106, 108, 111

aim of drive, 23, 24, 32, 33, 35, 39-40; in "emergence" view, 52-56; in parallelist view, 48

affection, *see* Tenderness

"afterwardsness," *see après-coup*

anaclisis/anaclitic, *see* leaning-on; leaning-on type of object-choice

anal stage; anality, 25, 36, 49, 53, 62, 69-72, 122

anatomy, 125-26

André, Jacques, 7, 13

"animalism," 123

animal migrations, 107

animal psychology, 60, 67, 88

animals, ideology and, 123-30

Anlehnung, see leaning-on

anxiety, 16-17

Anzieu, Didier, 6n, 73n, 79, 87, 88

après-coup (*Nachträglichkeit*; "afterwardsness"), xiin, 29-31, 38, 63

Aristophanes, 19-21, 23, 91, 104, 107

Aristotle, 105

association (*Vergesellschaftung*), 31, 50

attachment, 29, 64-66, 76, 92; model of (Model I), 93-99, 102, 104; *see also* leaning-on

"auto-," *see* self

autoerotism, 38-42, 48-50, 61-62, 82, 83, 85-86, 89, 94-96, 103

Azar, Amine A., 43n

Berman, Antoine, 30

bestial, the, 123-25, 124, 127

binding, 89-90, 93-95, 103, 105, 107, 110, 111, 130

"bio-ethics," 129

biologism, 11, 76, 98-99, 102, 106-7, 109, 110, 112, 123; Kleinian, 112

biologizing: in childhood sexual theories, 127; Kleinian, 112; use of term, 4, 12

biology: as ideology, 122-30; and thought processes, 115-16

biting, 70-71

Bourguignon, André, 15n

breast, 46, 50, 51, 56, 59, 60, 73-74, 76; as signifier, 59

Buddhism, 108

cannibalism, 55-56

care; caregiving, 57, 64-65, 71-73; *see also* tenderness

Cartesianism, 80

castration, 120, 125-27

"Chasse aux gènes, La," 118n

Chertok, Léon. 73

child: relation to adult of, 57, 122 (and see adult other); relation to object of (three models), 93-102; sexual theories of, 127; *see also* infantile sexuality; seduction

Chorier, Bénédicte, 124n

Christianity, 129

"cloacal" excitation, 13

cloacal theory, 127

co-excitation, 54, 69-760

Colette, 56n

concepts, implicit/para-, 29-32

"Confusion of Tongues between Adults and the Child" (Ferenczi), 66-67

conjunction, 50

contiguity/continuity in derivation, 37, 51, 59, 78

Cotet, Pierre, 15n

"cover formation" (*Deckbildung*), 209

Darwinism, neo-Darwinism, 18, 120

Dayan, Maurice, 110

death, wish for, 108-9

An Introduction," 4, 27, 61, 63-65, 67, 72, 76, 81, 84-86, 89n, 90-99; "On the Universal Tendency to Debasement in the Sphere of Love," 29n; "An Outline of Psycho-Analysis," 103-5; "Project for a Scientific Psychology," 66n, 73, 90; "The Psycho-Analytic View of Psychogenic Disturbances of Vision," 27; "Schreber Case," 81-85, 87n; *Standard Edition*, 14n, 27n, 63; *Three Essays on the Theory of Sexuality*, 14-16, 20-27, 31, 33, 37-41, 46-47, 53-54, 57, 62, 63, 86, 94, 104, 122; *Totem and Taboo*, 109, 120

Genesis, 128-29
genetics, 115, 118-22, 128, 130
genitality; genital zone, 24-26, 33n, 36, 39-40, 71-72
genitals as love-object, 83
genome, 118
Gestalt, 88; object as, 94-95
goal-directedness, 17, 18, 23-26, 82-83, 102, 107, 121, 122
going-astray, *see* Straying
Greek mythology, 124; *see also* Aristophanes
Green, André, 55-56
Gribinski, Michel, 22G
Grigg, Russell, 15n

Haeckel, Ernst, 9
hallucination, 51
hate, 91, 99, 110
Hegel, G. W. F., 7
herd instinct, 18
heredity, 14, 17, 18, 119-20; *see also* acquired/innate distinction; genetics; instinct; phlyogenesis
hermeneutics, 110-11
heterosexual object-choice, 83, 86
Hobbes, Thomas, 124-25
Hölderlin, Friedrich, 7
homosexuality, 83, 86, 119
hunger, 98-99

id, 11-12, 95, 125
identifications, ego and, 80-81
ideology, 122-30
implantation, 69, 73
imprinting, 66, 88, 120
incest prohibition, 127-28
incorporation, 54-56
individual, ego as, 77-78, 81
infantile sexuality, 22-25, 35-43, 56-58, 122
ingestion, 54-55
innate/acquired distinction, 118, 120-22; *see also* heredity
instinct (*Instinkt*): definition of, 17-22; versus "drive" (*Trieb*), 14-17, 107-8; sexual, 121
Instincts, Les (Viaud), 18
interaction, 68, 76
Isaacs, Susan, 42-43, 56

Jordan, Bertrand, 118n

Jealous Potter, The (Lévi-Strauss), 124
"Jeannot's knife," 33
Jaffrin, S., 12n
Jones, Ernest, 71n
Jung, Carl Gustav, 6, 35-36, 81, 97, 99-102

Kaës, René. 28n
"Karl Abraham: lecture de son oeuvre" (Rosolato and Widlöcher), 70
Klein, Melanie; Kleinians, 11, 42-43, 50, 73, 110-12
Krafft-Ebing, Richard von, 23
Koeppel, Philippe, 22n

La Fontaine, Jean de, 56n
Lacan, Jacques, 11, 15-16, 30, 33-34, 37 87-88, 109, 127
Lagache, Daniel, 29
Lamarckianism, 120
Lanouzière, Jacqueline, 72-73
Laplanche, Jean, works of: "The Derivation of Psychoanalytic Entities," 36-37, 78; "Interpréter [avec] Freud,"

135

6; *The Language of Psycho-Analysis* (with J.-B. Pontalis), 28-29, 50, 64, 77-78, 90-91; *Life and Death in Psychoanalysis*, 3, 9, 15n, 22n, 27n, 32, 36n, 47-48, 50 78, 105-6, 109; "Masochism and the General Theory of Seduction," 54n; *New Foundations for Psychoanalysis*, 3. 60; "Notes on Afterwardsness," 31n; *Problématiques I-VII*, xi, xiin; *Problématiques I: L'angoisse*, xiin, 89n; *Problématiques II: Castration et symbolisations*, xiin, 25n; *Problématiques III: La sublimation*, xiin, 15n, 32, 45, 89n; *Problématiques IV: L'inconscient et le ça/The Unconscious and the Id*, xiin, 15n, 45; *Problématiques V: Le baquet. Transcendance du transfert*, xiin, 101n; *Problématiques VI: l'après-coup*, xiin, 30n, 31n; *La pulsion our quoi faire?* (with Anzieu et al.), 73n; "Repenser Freud" (interview), 12n; "La soi-disant pulsion sexuelle," 125n; *Traduire Freud* (with Bourguignon et al.), 15n; "The Unfinished Copernican Revolution," 9, 51n, 72

leaning-on (*Anlehnung*, "anaclisis," "afterwardsness," propping), 3-4, 13, 27-32, 35, 45-53, 47, 50, 68-70; adult other and, 69; as "emergence," 47, 50-53, 59, 102; Kleinians and, 111; parallelist view of, 47-49, 52, 59; and seduction, 38, 73, 75-76, 94; three conceptions of, 46-47; use of term, 27n, 28n, 63

leaning-on ("anaclitic") type of object-choice, 63, 76, 90-92

Leonardo da Vinci, 81, 83, 89n

Léonardo da Vinci: mythologie ou théologie (Maïdani-Gérard), 89n

Lévi-Strauss, Claude, 123-24, 127

Lewin, Bertram, 55

libido, 35-36, 81-82, 84, 89-90, 95-100

life drives, 15, 19-22, 33n, 61, 92, 103, 107, 110; *see also* Eros

lips, 46-48, 53

love, 64-66, 89-92, 97-99, 103, 110, 111

Macey, David, 3n

"Mme K... interpréta" (Dayan), 110

Maïdani-Gérard, J.-P., 89n

"Malédiction des pharaons, La" (Azar), 43n

Mandel, Gérard, 43n

Marx, Karl, 7

masochism, 54, 69

Masson, Jeffrey Moussaïeff, 14n

masturbation, 27-28, 41-42, 56-57

materialism, 115-16

Mehlman, Jeffrey, 3n, 27n, 36n

metabiological plane, 106-7, 112

metabolization, 37, 50, 55, 106

metaphor, 51, 52, 54-55; ego and, 78-81

metonymy: object and, 51, 52, 59; ego and, 78-81

milk, 46, 50, 51, 59-62, 76

mind-body split, 12, 13

mirror image, 87n, 89n

mirror stage (Lacan), 87-88, 89n

"Mirror Stage as Formative of the I Function, The" (Lacan), 87

Mitsou (Colette), 56n

Moebius, Paul Julius, 23

Moll, Albert, 23

mother, 46, 51, 57, 60-61, 64-65, 69, 71-72, 76, 78, 81, 83, 94, 121, 128

mucous membranes, 53

myth, 4, 22, 87n, 98, 123-30; *see also* Aristophanes

narcissism, 66, 76, 81-86, 89-92, 102-4; model of (Model III), 93-99, 108; as moments, not stage, 86; primary / secondary, 84-86, 89n; psychosis and, 84; self-preservation absorbed by, 97-100; as stage, 102-3

narcissistic object-choice, 83, 89-92

Nahrungszufuhr/Nahrungseinfuhr, 72

"Nature and Function of Phantasy, The," (Isaacs), 42-43

Freud';s theory of, 3, 4n, 12-14, 30-31, 119; general theory of, xii, 122, 123, 126-27, 130; leaning-on and 38, 73, 94, 75-76

self, 80-83, 93

"self" phase of drive, 48-49, 90, 106

self-preservation; self-preservation drives, 3-4, 13, 16, 18, 26-29, 31-32, 65, 67, 76, 97, 121; attachment model and, 93-94; Kleinians and, 111; narcissistic sexuality and, 97-101; sexual drive and, 26-29, 31-32, 45-64, 67-68, 73, 121; tenderness and, 65-69

sensuality, affection vs., 65

sexual instinct, 121

sexuality; sexual drive, 17n, 22, 27-28, 95; biologizing of, 12-13, 19; "erotic," 94; four aspects of, 32-35; Kleinians and, 111; self-preservation and, 26-29, 31-32, 45-64, 67-68, 73, 121; *see also* libido

"Ship of Theseus," 65

signifier, 13, 59, 72, 110

skin-ego (Anzieu), 88

source of drive, 23, 32-35, 39-40, 47-49,73, 95; in "emergence" view, 51-54, 56, 73; as exogenous, 55

source-object, 8-9, 73

sphincter control, 71, 72

Spiegelung (mirror image), 87n

Spinoza, Baruch, 116

spiral, the, xi, xii, 9

stage(s); stageism, 25-26, 36, 69-72, 81, 86, 87, 122; narcissism as, 102-3; *see also* specific stages

Stekel, Wilhelm, 41

stool; feces, 51, 62, 71

Strachey, James, 27, 63, 121

straying/going-astray (*le fourvoiement*), xi, xii, 3-5, 7-9, 11-14, 75, 76, 85, 93, 102-398, 110; with deat drive, 107-10; Instinkt and, 19, 22; Kleinians and, 43, 110-12; and leaning-on, 27, 31-32, 52; seduction theory and, 13-14, 31, 32

structuralism, 11, 127-28

sublimation, 32

sucking, 46, 49, 65; as stage, 70-71

superego, 77

"Symbolic, the" (Lacan), 127

symbolization, 37, 48-51, 53, 59

Symposium (Plato), 19-21

teleology, 32-33n; *see also* goal-directedness

tenderness 57, 65-67, 69, 76, 91

thought processes, 115-16

Thurston, Luke, 9n, 45n, 54n

toilet training, 72

totemism, 123-24

Totemism (Lévi-Strauss), 124

translation, test of, 30

"tub," psychoanalytic, 101n, 111

unbinding, 105-7, 110, 111

unconscious, 66-67, 112; "life" and "death" in, 109; as preceding consciousness, 43

urethral/urinary stage, 36, 62, 71

Viaud, Gaston, 18

Vienna Psychoanalytical Society, 27-28, 41-42, 57-57, 65, 67

Wallon, Henri, 87

Widlöcher, Daniel, 70, 73n

wolf, 124-25

Zärtlichkeiten, 57, 65, 69

Ziel (aim), 32-33n

Zweck (goal), 17, 32-33n, 107

The Unconscious in Translation

The mission of UIT is to publish translations of French texts in the areas of psychoanalysis and the philosophy of mind, important works that have not and likely would not otherwise soon be made available to English-language readers.

The Publisher and General Editor

Jonathan House teaches in the Institute for Comparative Literature and Society and in the Center for Psychoanalytic Training and Research, both at Columbia University. He practices psychiatry and psychoanalysis in New York City.

The Translator

In the areas of psychology and psychoanalysis, Donald Nicholson-Smith has translated Jean Piaget, Henri Wallon, Bärbel Inhelder, Jacques Derrida, and, notably, *The Language of Psycho-Analysis* by J.-B. Pontalis and Jean Laplanche. For UIT, he recently translated J.-B. Pontalis's *Brother of the Above*.